LET GO AND LET GOD

LET GO

AND LET GOD

Steps in Victorious Living

BY ALBERT E. CLIFFE

Prentice-Hall, Inc.

Englewood Cliffs, N. J.

Designed by Stefan Salter

30   29

DEDICATED

To the Rev. Norman E. Peterson, B.A., L.Th., rector of the Church of St. Columba, Montreal, through whose kindness and inspiration these *Lessons in Living* were first presented to the public.

Contents ⌒

CONTENTS

Introduction

THE Bible says, "In the world ye shall have tribulation." How much we have seen of this in the past few decades, with wars, more wars, and the promise of still another war to come. These and all our tribulations have come upon us simply because we have not lived up to the laws of God.

We have had the Christian Faith for two thousand years, and yet today we see the whole Christian world divided into sects, warring with and criticizing each other. We have refused the basic teaching of Jesus Christ that we love one another, we have refused to learn how to get along with each other, and hence we see nations unable to live together in any way at all.

The Bible has taught us, however, in a wonderful way, the answer to all the problems that life can throw at each of us from day to day. In other words, you, my reader, can possess within you a feeling that makes you the master of life, that will enable you to walk successfully through all the vicissitudes of life with peace of mind, with hope, and constant courage to face whatever trials may come your way.

By means of faith in a living Christ, a resurrected Christ, you can gain such security that nothing can ever defeat you, no sickness can ever overwhelm you, and by the practice of this faith you can learn to gain victory over life and death.

As a bee needs a hive, a bird needs its nest, and a ship a harbor in time of storm, so do we every day of our lives need a refuge in time of stress and trouble. This refuge is faith. Your religion, your trying to live according to the laws shown us by Jesus Christ, will give you that radiant, vibrant, living refuge.

The true purpose of religion in our lives is to give us the means with which to replace fear, our worst enemy; we need today not merely a formal dogmatic religion, but a religion that does things rather than merely thinks them. This kind of religion is just as real at 7 a.m. on Thursday as it is at 11 a.m. on Sunday.

Every man and woman in these troublous times needs something to hang onto every hour of the day—so that he or she can know how to handle every difficulty which can ever face them. Faith in a living Christ within us teaches us how to *let go and let God.*

This book has been written by a layman who by means of simple faith has found God, and who has surrendered everything to God. From the pages of this book you will glean the basic ideas of how to get along with people in every walk of life, and how to overcome your trials, your fears, your past and your future.

Life becomes a daily thrilling experience when the love of

[x]

God radiates from our hearts, for then the Christ within us radiates in our words, our appearance, our hands, and we see Christ in everyone we meet.

When we *let go and let God* we have the key to glorious living, and what is far more important—the key to an eternity with God.

Albert E. Cliffe

LET GO AND LET GOD

Let Go and Let God ~

WHEN you have been through a period of worry and tension, it is usually the practice of your doctor to have you take a vacation in some quiet restful spot where you can relax completely, forget your past worries and gain strength.

Very few people today know how to relax, they live in a world of rushing hither and yon. Each day is filled with work, engagements and no time for relaxation. Even when people take time off to go to a movie they usually want an exciting one, thus gaining more excitement for their already overworked nervous systems.

The average man at business is a good example of high tension living. If successful, he tries daily to better his past successes. The excitement of greater successes keeps him in constant tension, and fatigue remains unnoticed until he is in a complete state of mental exhaustion. The busy doctor, teacher, stenographer are good examples of high tension living. These people find that after they retire to bed their active minds will not let them rest, but they go on planning further ideas for the following days.

The rearing of children and providing meals for the family each night takes its toll from the nerves of the dependable mother. She becomes irritable, she cannot get rest even when she retires to bed, and sooner or later she has to seek medical advice to quiet her nerves.

We have nowadays all kinds of machinery in the home to save work, to save drudgery, but they have not in any way relieved the sense of nervous strain of the householder; in other words, we are all trying to burn the candle at both ends. *We do not know how to let go our anxieties.*

In this present century man has forgotten how to live, how to enjoy the simple things of life: the sunshine, the garden, quiet walks along country lanes. All of us every day look over our budgets, our costs in living, our economies, but few count the costs of life in terms of nervous expenditures.

Take the average man and woman of our present civilization, as soon as trouble comes, as soon as some little thing goes wrong—what do they do? They reach for a cigarette, a sure sign of nervous trouble, for they have become used to the solace of this potent drug. Many times we find people who suffer terrific pains in certain organs of their bodies, and when the doctor examines them he finds not a single thing organically wrong with them. Nerves, nervous tensions can bring tremendous amounts of real pain to every one of us. After years of struggling with life, we have never learned how to *let go our tensions and fears.*

Many children become nervous types because their parents

give them too much attention, too much personal worry about non-essentials, too much being cared for and being watched over. The causes of overactive nervous systems are many, so the doctors tell us, but among these causes we must claim that the worst causes of all are our constant rush and the complexity of the way we think and live.

In spite of the worries of everyday life, we must always keep before our minds the utter need for us to relax, to get rest and healthy sleep. Complete relaxation is the sure remedy for this thing called nervousness. Worry about the little and big things of life, worry about things which you fear may happen to you in the future, all tend to bring about tension. Worry becomes a real habit and if constantly practiced can bring about physical death after much suffering. What can you do about it? Learn to relax, learn to face the tribulations of life without fear, stop crossing bridges ahead of time, for worry is the interest you pay on trouble before it comes.

Show me a worrying person and I will show you a person who does not know how to relax.

Our religious faith, Christianity, shows us the complete answer to nervous troubles and tensions. A single constant affirmation that the everlasting arms of God are holding you up, repeated hour by hour until you become convinced that God is now your guide and stay, will often bring you out of worries and fears, but how many Christians will really *let go* their fears *and let God* handle them?

Suppose that you have a broken watch and you take it to a watchmaker, asking him if he can repair it. He takes out his glass and looks at the works and says that he most assuredly can repair it. Suppose then that you say to him, "Thank you," place it back in your purse or pocket and leave the store. Will you get that watch repaired? Most certainly not, for you have to leave the watch with the watchmaker.

It is just the same with your religious life. You have to get into the habit of leaving your troubles with God. The only complete and sure cure for your bad nerves, as you call them, is to relax in the hands of God and know that He is now looking after your troubles, that He is now guiding you into the quiet waters of inner peace.

If you have a poor tire on your car, what do you do? You can drive more carefully than ever, avoid the bad roads, the side and gravel roads, keeping to the main highways. So it is with your body. If your organs have withstood very badly indeed the wear and tear of life, then you must learn to take care of them until you gain that complete healing which can only come from a real, earnest practice of your religion. To him that believeth, all things are possible, says the Bible; but how many Christians really try to believe this statement?

The most wonderful thing that ever happened to me was this: many years ago *I let go* my past *and let God* take over my life. When I completely surrendered my life to Him, I lost my temper, my fears, my years of deadly illness and sicknesses. It meant facing life every hour with the truth that was in me to replace the negative thinking of a lifetime.

It meant an hourly contact with God, in the street car, the bus, my own car, my laboratory—no matter where I went I had an appointment with Him. What came of it? Peace of mind, health and spiritual prosperity.

Are you willing, friend, after reading this chapter to-day, to find God? Are you willing to put Him first in your life? Are

[4]

you willing to *let go, and let* God be your mentor from this day on?

Then if you are, you, too, can have no fears, no tensions, no nervousness, no worries. When you take His yoke upon you, your life is a converted one. No longer do the sins of the devil haunt you, no longer can the so-called powers of evil assail you, but you learn to live happily, healthfully, confidently, because having *let go,* you *let* God and abundant living come into your life.

Believing in Life ♒

I BELIEVE with all my heart and soul that God our Father wants us, His children, to live happy, healthful lives, and I believe that my religion, the Christian Faith, is the only answer for us, for a more abundant life. Jesus taught us that He came to bring this more abundant life, not in terms of millions of dollars, not in forms of wealth, but in that peace of mind which is the secret of successful living.

We live burdened with the cares of life, and even our so-called pleasures take their toll out of our nervous systems—which amounts to a tremendous tax on our daily strength. We expend our mental energies so much that it is no wonder so many thousands of people are tired, discouraged, and sick to the point of death.

If you drive, you know that your battery must not be over-taxed; it needs recharging often if the strain of its daily work is too great. So our human batteries are filled with power for us to use, but only as long as we obey the rules and never waste our energies. Each of us is made up of mind, body and soul; each vital to the other, each essential to the harmonious running of the whole.

Peace of mind is the greatest asset we can have for happy, healthy living. This is an inner victory which only comes from knowing God intimately. Then the material things of life do not bother us any longer—we live in a spiritual world, and spiritual values are the only real values in life.

We each have this power within us and when we learn by faith to control this power, then we know how to use it, how to liberate it for our daily needs.

A lady came to me recently with a serious problem and said to me, "How I would like to get away from it all, how I would like to end my life." I showed her another case I had come across the same day, far worse than hers; far more dreadful things to face than she had ever had to face. I showed her how this lady had got out of her fearful condition. She at once saw my point, was sorry for her selfishness and accepted Christ from then on. She began to recover at once, her pains left. Her fears had gone with that inner faith that God was now working for her betterment. She had always put the emphasis in her life on the negative side of things, and when she got the positive uppermost, then she gained the victory.

The answer to all our problems of living is how we face them, not where we were born, not that we have had a poor environment, not that we had no chance of an education. The answer is always within ourselves. Fighting, struggling against life will never win us a victory. You have to make your own inner consciousness a citadel of peace, knowing that

Christ lives there. You become a member of the D.W.C.—
Don't Worry Club—leaving your worries to Him.

We all need a safety valve every day of our lives, and we find
it in our religion. Christ is the safety valve for your emotions,
your wrong thinking. You cannot have a nervous condition
when you open this safety valve.

When your body shows illness and fatigue, it is time you
looked into the matter. You must find out what has been
wrong with your way of living, what sins are dominating you,
what hates and criticisms are controlling your mind. You must
sit down and see how to gain mastery over these things. You
must admit them, and learn to meditate with God, who will
give you a glorious victory over everything that has upset you
in your past life.

When you show love to your fellowmen, even to those who
have hurt you, when you give service and money to your fellowmen, to your church, then you are in a positive state of
mind. If you are, however, dominated by the opposites, hate,
discord, resentment, criticism, then these forces, being negative, will tear you down and bring you suffering, poverty, and
complete failure in life. Negative states of thinking bring nervousness and nervous breakdowns, which no mere electric
shock treatment at any hospital will ever cure. The little an-
noyances of your life are what bring about your greatest troubles. Little things you say "get on your nerves"—this shows
you are a negative thinker, you have no faith in God, even
though you do go to church and recite a dozen creeds.

Negative thinking will always lead to failure and nervous
prostration; but positive faith—positive thinking—will lead
you towards happy, healthy and abundant living.

[9]

The positive way of life is the Jesus Christ way—it is always the right way. Look at the face of a Salvation Army lass, radiant with inner peace, joyful, no color on those cheeks from a drug store. She has been to God's beauty parlor; she has gotten that permanent which is a permanent for enternity. Wouldn't you like to have that radiance which comes from knowing the Master? Would you not love to be able to sing with her, "Nothing but the blood of Jesus can ever wash away my sins"? She knows Jesus from a daily contact with Him, by a surrender to Him. She believes in life—yes indeed, life everlasting.

Religion is and must ever be the basis of life, the key to the armory of your soul. Its mission is to provide a channel whereby God's spiritual powers may come into your life and mine, to stop us from resisting those things which irritate us daily. To give us trust in our fellowman, to take away all our tensions and to work so that our bodies are not only healed of sickness, but are speeded up. How can you get this peace? Through confidence in the promises of Jesus Christ. Develop this confidence daily as you would learn how to play a piano. Constant hourly practice is essential. *Thou wilt keep him in perfect peace whose mind is stayed on Thee.*

This then is why I believe in life. I know in Whom I have believed, I came to Him, I saw Him, I conquered all things that had prevented my knowing Him before.

I believe most assuredly that Jesus came to bring us a life more abundant; I believe that trying to live is life; by following His precepts every hour of my life, I too shall know the joys of peaceful living, knowing that all my needs will be provided for until the day when He comes to take me to His eternal home.

[10]

What are the precepts *you* must follow to know the more abundant life? The next ten chapters will explain to you the faults of your thinking—the way to change your life from negative to positive. I like to call these my *ten steps in victorious living.*

In them you can find the key to what has been wrong with your personality. By improving your personality—by learning what God's laws are for you—you can learn to live so that you will have the health and happiness you need.

THE FIRST STEP IS

Getting Along
with People ⟋ᴬᵗᵗ

"Thou wilt keep him in perfect peace, whose mind is stayed on Thee."—Isaiah 26:3.

THE most important basis for successful living is the art of knowing how to get along with people, how to adjust ourselves from day to day to the different temperaments we meet in our relatives and our friends, how to see the good in them and in their actions and how to ignore the evil they sometimes do to us.

The Bible distinctly tells us that God will keep any man or woman inwardly at peace and in goodwill when that person fixes his mind, his thoughts and his actions, not on material things, not on resentment, criticism and antagonism, but on God.

Therefore, to get along with people, we first of all have to learn how to control our thoughts. There was never a time in the world's history when men needed to know how to get along with people, more than at the present time. Many years ago, men who could not adjust themselves to life could get away into far countries and live alone, finding a home for themselves in the wilderness, in the forest or on a lonely island. In this way they did not have to associate with people, and their negative personalities began eventually adjusting to nature. Today, as one writer has said, "there are no islands any more."

Every man and every woman wants happiness and harmony in life, but if we are constantly upset by the doings of our relatives and associates, we cannot have this harmony. Therefore we must learn how to win the friendship and respect of others, and we must learn how to gain their co-operation every day of our lives. We may be geniuses in some particular way, but unless we have discovered the secret of getting along with people, we will never enjoy successful living.

To be a happy person does not depend upon who we are, it does not depend upon education, it is not just a question of brains; basically it is how we react to people and to conditions every day. We often judge people by the car they drive or the clothing they wear; but remember that we may see a man outside a theater dressed like an admiral who probably never saw the sea and does not even know how to row a boat.

Anyone at any time can interest people, can influence them and lead them the way he wants them to go. If you are one of those people who say they do not care what others think about them, then I venture to make this statement: you are putting on a pose; inwardly you *do* care, because we all like to be able to win friends and influence people.

When we were born, God gave us all the tools we need for successful living, but first of all we have to know how to use them in order to get what we want from life. There are three factors involved: first, yourself; second, other people; and third, methods to follow.

First of all, do you know yourself? Do you recognize and admit your weaknesses? Have you tried to overcome them? Do you suffer from an inferiority complex? Are you timid, lazy, selfish, hot-tempered, cynical, critical, mean, jealous, sarcastic or conceited? These are the little sins that go into the making of your character. We find that so many people think because they do not break any of the Ten Commandments, then there are no other sins to worry about. But there are thousands of little errors in our thinking and in our actions which definitely mold our character negatively. These are sins because in practicing them we are putting them before God and this is breaking the first commandment which says, "Thou shalt have no other gods before Me."

A young lady came to work for me in my laboratory. She was a graduate chemist, had taken a household science course at a university, and previous to that she had taken a complete stenographic course. She was extremely shy. She had tried several religious faiths, but basically she never knew what she wanted to be and she certainly did not know herself.

In a park in Toronto, one noon hour, she came across a tract on "How to Know Yourself." She read it all on that park bench; she found herself because the tract opened her eyes to her weakness, and at the same time she found God. She changed her life; from that moment she decided to give herself to mission work in which she became very happy, successful and well able to get along with people.

If only we would learn every day of our lives to overcome those things in our character which are negative, to *let go and*

[15]

let God take them over, we would all know what it was to experience harmonious living.

What do you believe about yourself? Have you always been a yes man in your place of employment? To be successful you have to learn to have a mind of your own, to have the courage of your own convictions—for this gives you stability of character. I come across many people in my work who are afraid of facing life because they are filled with the idea that they are failures.

There are thousands of people in offices, factories and stores who have no idea of where they are going from here, who are dissatisfied with their jobs and unable to get along with people. The man or woman whom you do not like in your place of employment has many good points. In disliking them, you can only see their bad points, the evil in them. But before you start criticizing other people you should see that there are no bad points in you.

Have you ever realized that God allows us to live a lifetime on this earth, and in that time He never once criticizes or condemns us? He gave us brains, a free will, talents, and a book of rules to follow, the Bible. If with all this material we cannot find ourselves, then the fault does not lie in our environment, the fault does not lie in God, the fault lies within ourselves.

I met a man some time ago, married and father of three children. This man was everlastingly seeking something he could not find. He devoted five nights a week to his church and his lodge, which placed a tremendous load upon his wife. This in turn brought about her breakdown, followed by doctor's bills and other expenses. One morning he opened the Bible at the text at the head of this chapter. He thought about those words all day. That night he surrendered himself completely to God, he *let go and let God.* He realized that the load he had given his wife to bear for some years was unjust. He now spends his nights at home helping with the housework and the raising of his children. He learned how to get along with his family for the first time, and he gained that inner peace which radiated in a healthy wife, a happy home, increased ideas in his business life, and successful living.

As we go through life every day, we meet many types of people, good people, bad people; some we like at once and some we dislike the instant we meet them. This is the sort of thing that other people find in you. So if you want to gain favor with other people you must first of all build a personality of your own and then you must have a sympathetic tolerance of the other person's point of view.

There is no doubt but that by adjusting ourselves to others, by being considerate of the things in their characters which annoy us, that we build our own character. Dolly Madison, wife of President James Madison, was asked one day how she gained such power over people. She replied, "I have no power over anyone. I merely made up my mind to love everyone, to see their good points, and in return these people see the good points in me and learn to love me."

Now, friend, if you are the critical, fault-finding type, if you are super-sensitive to the things you have to face each day, I can assure you this will bring you no friendships whatsoever. These are faults in your character which you must learn to control and overcome.

I often think that the successful salesman or saleswoman has something called *You*point—he or she understands immediately *your* viewpoint and handles you accordingly. One of the first rules we have to learn in order to get along with people is to talk to others about themselves and their habits, their sports and the things they like to do, instead of always talking about our own selves. In this way we learn how to practice cheerfulness, tact, sympathy and gratitude.

St. Paul said, "I can do all things through Christ which strengtheneth me." Do you believe this statement? If so, then why don't you apply it? Life to us all is simply a series of adventures, a series of every-day lessons in living. We must learn day by day how to develop this thing called character, how to overcome the things we seem to have inherited from our forefathers. We do this through our minds, by changing the patterns of our thinking, by becoming positive instead of negative thinkers.

If you will start off the day, as you leave your home in the morning, believing that through Christ and His power within you, you can do all the things you have to face that particular day, you will gain a wonderful conviction of the power which resides within you.

In our daily life we come across many people who show jealousy towards us. Please remember that no one in this world is ever jealous of a fool and that no one can hurt you unless you let them, by fearing them. If you are the type of person who is kind to some people, but an entirely different person to others, then you are two-faced and unstable in many ways. By the law of return you will receive in later years this same treatment from others that you have given people in the earlier part of your life.

It is a strange thing about religion that many people appear to love spending Sunday with God, but oh how they balk at having Him as an everyday guest in their homes or places of employment. Next to God the most important person for you to know is self, your own self. Don't you know that, as a Christian, life was meant for you by God to be a happy experience, certainly not a miserable one. Successful living does not mean accumulating material things, it means inner peace of mind; it means that gift of being able to adjust oneself to everyone else; it also means that all your needs for daily living will be taken care of by God.

Some years ago I had a stenographer who had occupied seven jobs in four years. She was very good-looking but I discovered she was a flirt; she was very vain, snobbish and sarcastic. She definitely had the idea that she could get any man she wanted. She was not interested in her work or her remarkable talents. She was really a selfish and very emotional type. I quickly learned her weak points, at the same time showing her the capacity she had for her particular work. I made her dress more plainly for the office. In a very short time she changed her thinking patterns and began to study books which she saw in my office dealing with the power of thought. At a church meeting one night she gave herself to God. Shortly after that she met the right man and is now a very great help to her husband in his duties. But it was not until she found God, the indwelling Christ, that she found herself. Finding yourself invariably means finding God.

Are you afraid of being called religious? You don't have to show your religion to people by the carrying of a Bible, by dressing in dark clothes, by always having a long face—but you do show your religious convictions by the way you react to people. Many people think that when they accept religion they are going to have to give up many of the things in life which gave them pleasure. Let me assure you that when you find Christ you don't have to give up anything good, because the wrong things in life automatically give you up and you are led into a wonderful enjoyment, the joy of living.

You show your religious convictions by the things you do and say each day, by how you live. You never show them by argument, because every man and every woman has the inborn right to worship God in his own way. Many so-called Christians are miserable, fearful, sick; they just do not know how to apply the teachings of Jesus. Oh yes, they can quote the Bible from cover to cover; they rejoice in telling you how many years they have been saved. But in so many cases these same people know only the letter of the law; they have never learned how to apply the simple teachings of the Master to everyday living, so they do not get along with themselves and invariably get along with no one else. We must learn every day how to study people, how to learn their likes and dislikes and how to cater to them.

In my work in industry I never hesitated to give a pat on the back to the man or woman who did a good job each day, because they always reacted marvelously to my compliments. So many employers are afraid to do this because they fear that if they do, these people will immediately demand an increase in salary, but I have never found this to be the case. When your newsboy, in all kinds of weather, delivers your newspaper with promptness; when your baker and milkman face the storms of winter to supply your needs; when your postman has to face every kind of discomfort to bring your mail; do you think of rewarding these people with a word, a smile or maybe a little gift or tip of some kind? Every time someone does something for you, no matter how small it may be, see that you in return give something to them or to someone else, for this is what makes the world go round. The secret of harmonious living is all in knowing how.

The Bible teaches us that everyone on this earth, Catholic or Protestant, Jew or Gentile, men of every creed and every color, are sons of God. In the Christian Faith we are told that we are heirs to all that God has made; that within us is the Kingdom of Heaven. Have you found this Kingdom? If you have, then you know what it is to have harmony, health and happiness in life. You have gained the art of knowing how to overcome your sins, your sicknesses and your fears.

One gets a marvelous feeling of power when he practices the magic of believing in Jesus Christ, because he then knows that he is heir to joy, eternal joy. We live this life to prepare us for that wonderful life to come. Eternity does not start for you and me when we go through that physical stage called death. It started for us the day we were born, and whatever we make of our lives every day is what we shall reap in the ages which are to come.

Friend, life is a constant overcoming, for the Bible says that in this world we shall have tribulations, but think what thrill and joy there is in overcoming every day some problem which faces you and has defeated you in the past. And with your consciousness of the Christ within, you can overcome all things.

What particular sin is in your physical make-up? What particular weakness? Try to find out after reading this chapter. Know that you can get rid of those negative conditions the minute you try to find the Christ by simply believing that what Jesus said was true. Through faith in Him and what He did for you some two thousand years ago, you can become a new person. Study the Bible every day, believe your Bible every day and let no one at any time destroy your faith in it. To be able to master a piano, to be able to play a good game of golf or tennis requires daily practice, and so does your religion—*everyday practice*. Jesus gave us two commandments to follow: put God first in your life, and your fellowman before yourself. Surely, friend, it is not too hard to keep these commandments. So many people have the right aim in life, but they never seem to pull the trigger. Is this *your* fault? What aim have you got in life, and what have you done about using your religion to bring it about?

John the Baptist, we are told, baptized with water but Jesus baptized with the Holy Spirit. Yet He did not give to us this baptism until He had been crucified. The Holy Spirit received by the hundred and twenty people at Pentecost is ready for you, but cannot be received by you until you are ready to receive it. If you will not consent to give up those things in your make-up which are wrong, then you are not ready to receive the gift. If your prayers remain unanswered, you have your foot on the hose, for you have not yet completely surrendered to Him the wrongs and sins of your life. Jesus Christ redeems us today and He will make the best even out of your worst "past."

He more than forgives you. He will turn your troubles and your liabilities into assets. He will make your self-made hells into Heaven. No matter how you have suffered from sickness, no matter how much you have messed up your life, you can this very moment turn over this mess in absolute faith. It has been said, "He unmesses the messer and makes an asset of the mess." Jesus took an uneducated fisherman and, after living with him daily for three years, this poor fisherman became the writer of a Gospel which revolutionized the world. The Christ can take almost nothing and make it almost everything. It is the Christ who brings to us today a full and perfect salvation, and full and perfect healing from sin and from sickness. Friend, will you not therefore believe?

Test Him and see if you can prove Him even as you read this book. Remember that the longer you stay away from your adventure of finding the Christ, the longer you will live in sickness and poverty and need. I can assure you that the Christ lives in each man and each woman, and we can find Him if we will only believe.

To get along with people, to have the art of knowing how, we must first find God. In finding ourselves we find Him. This will bring us the true and lasting happiness which was the gift of Jesus Christ to men.

THE SECOND STEP IS

Freeing Yourself
from Fear

"Love your enemies . . . do good to them
that hate you."—*St. Matthew 5:44.*

To GET along in life we must know something about
this thing called human nature. It is the cause of all things
which will come to each of us, and the reason we will react to
them as we do. If someone makes us angry, if someone does a
wrong deed against us, if someone does a good deed towards
us or makes us a gift of some kind, the manner in which we
react to all these things is always determined by our own particular nature.

For instance, the slow phlegmatic person always takes
things calmly and is not very easily ruffled, while the sensitive
person is a nervous type and gets ruffled very quickly and goes
off on tangents.

Now the best way to make a friend of anyone is to appeal
to some characteristic he possesses. Try to learn how to understand the various characteristics of your friends and associates. Find out what things they like and what things they

[25]

dislike and watch day by day how they react to the circumstances of life.

What is your reaction when a street-car driver slams the door in your face just as you get there? Do you call him all kinds of names, do you say and think how unkind he was? Do you write to the company about his wrong treatment of you? This is entirely wrong, and if you want people to like you, you must first of all learn to like people, no matter what they may do to you. Learn how to overlook the things you dislike in them, see their good points and magnify those points.

There is no doubt that the secret of good living is basically how to know and understand yourself. The events of every day in the business world are often of a disturbing nature, but if you allow these things to depress you, then you have not learned how to understand human nature. It is a fact that if you do not get along with people, you either do not like people or you are definitely afraid of them.

Many years ago I worked under a manager who was very hard to understand. All the employees in every department were very much afraid of him. Then one day I discovered that his main hobby was the study of Egyptology, and I approached him, being interested in the same subject, to ask him if he would lend me two of the books in his library. He was very surprised to find out that I was interested in this subject and that I had once written a thesis upon it. From that day on I had no fear of him and we became great friends. I discovered a characteristic common to both of us, and through an understanding of human nature I solved this problem.

In another company which employed me, the president, who was very wealthy, had a mania for neatness and a terrific hatred of wastage. One day while going to his office with the manager under whom I worked, the president noticed a pin on the floor and told the manager to pick up that pin, as he might need it some day. It was very humiliating, of course, to the manager, to have been so spoken to in front of me, his junior. Some time later it was my job to see the president in connection with some concessions we wanted from him relative to a sales convention, and as I sat down in his office, I picked a pin from the floor and placed it on the pin tray on his desk. He immediately reacted by saying, "Well, I am glad to know that my chief chemist does not waste pins any more than I do." I gained every point which I wanted from that time on. Needless to say, there was no pin on the floor, for I had carried that pin in my hand before approaching him. I knew his characteristics and through that little experiment I was able to overcome the arguments which otherwise he would have presented to me; in other words, he learned to like me because he discovered something in me of which he approved.

The young child has only three emotions when he is born into this world, fear, rage and love, but as he goes through life he gets many more emotional complexes, some of which he learns how to control and some of which, unfortunately, control him.

We gain many fears which have no existence in reality at all. Maybe when you look from a bridge to a river below you are overcome with nausea. When you come suddenly face to face with a situation you did not expect, when a serious sickness of some kind overtakes you, fear is the thing that dominates your mind. You must learn to face the thing you fear or you will be a defeated person.

It was my job on one occasion to call on the brothers in one of the monasteries in the Province of Quebec, and as I parked my car I saw a huge mastiff with a heavy fifty-foot chain tied to his neck. There was a big sign in French saying, "Beware of the Dog!" He was very savage indeed, but having no fear of animals, I walked up to him, speaking to him gently in French. Gradually his ears dropped and he lay on the ground and I got close to him. He suddenly jumped up, put his big paws on my shoulders and started to lick my face. At this moment one of the monks came up from the barn. He was terrified because he thought the dog was about to eat me. But I had conquered the dog by showing no fear, only love. Before keeping my appointment, I drove down to the village and brought him some bones. On every monthly visit to the monastery that dog knew the sound of my engine, and as my car drove into the yard his ears would be pricked up, his tail wagging, and he would bark joyfully because he knew he had a friend in that car.

How do you react when you hear some mean remark made by someone about you? When someone borrows your things without permission? When someone enters your desk in your absence? How do you react when your boss tells you to do a job because someone else shirked it? It is knowing the answer to these problems in a positive way, knowing human nature, that makes you know how to get along in life.

This emotion called love teaches you many things, for you have to practice love every hour of the day when living with people. Love in your nature will make people want to agree with you. It will make you want to associate with people who think as you do, who have the same religious views as you have. Love will make you want to do things for others. Fear is one of the strongest emotions with which to influence people. Take the old-fashioned evangelist with his threats of a fiery hell in the afterlife. Take the patent medicine manufacturer who states that if you do not use his product you will suffer from various hideous diseases. Unfortunately much of the advertising in our magazines today has a fear background. The vitamin advertisements we have seen for years were designed in many cases to appeal to our fears.

You must try to learn day by day how to understand human emotions, and learn to identify people by their reaction to these emotions; but first of all learn how you yourself react to them. Once you solve these investigations, you will understand human nature perfectly.

Samson was the strongest man in the Bible, and able to accomplish wonderful deeds, until a certain day. That day was the day he didn't keep his mouth shut and gave away the secret of his strength. This applies to you. If you want to live successfully you have to learn to keep your mouth shut. God gave you two ears and one mouth, so that you could listen to twice as much as you say.

By quoting someone incorrectly, by passing on a confidence, by misunderstanding a remark, you can cause oceans of trouble for yourself. You must learn when to speak and when to keep your mouth shut. Human nature is the thing that makes some men hewers of wood and other men drawers of dividends. We all have the same kind of brain. We all have the divine right of free will. We all have the power of thought, but it is according to our human nature that we attain successful living.

How many Christians today try to see the Christ in the people they have to get along with? Are you full of criticism for people who belong to churches other than the one you attend? One lady I met told me that she often spent three hours a day in prayer with God, but she never got the answer to her prayers. She was a very sick person, and a very self-righteous one, for she said she never broke any of the Ten Commandments. She detested her next-door neighbor because he went to a certain church; in fact, no one was going to Heaven except those who belonged to her little sect. I eventually managed to convince her of the wickedness of her criticism of others. When she asked God's forgiveness for those things and really believed she had received that forgiveness, she gained a healing from her diseases. We must get an inner conviction of the power that is within us.

In the Christian Faith we are told to love our enemies, to pray for them that curse us, and to do good to them that hate us. This means that forgiveness is the basic teaching of the Christian Faith. As Jesus forgave the men who tortured and crucified Him, how much easier it is for you to forgive those who wrong you every day. Without this forgiveness on your part, you will never attain happy living. Jesus knew the secret of how to get along with people, and He taught us how to do it also. He sensed the personality, the inner thoughts of everyone He met, and you can do this too. There is no room in your heart for fear and worry of any kind when you are a Christian, for then you know and apply in your daily living the truth that makes you free. If you do not control your emotions, or if fear of some kind dominates your life, you can without doubt look forward to diseases coming to you later in life.

The one technique to apply is to develop faith through Jesus Christ. To affirm every hour positive thoughts; to know God is ever aware of you, ever beside you.

A short time ago, while driving in a taxi, an imminent collision with another car became apparent, due to the other driver coming out of a side street at a terrific speed. I had no fear, I relaxed completely; not for the crash which was to come but for the crash which was not to come. I knew that God was in our car and as we pulled up a little further along the street, the taxi driver, with perspiration running down his face, said, "God was in my car tonight." This gave me a chance to explain to him how he had proved God by the experience and how he could prove Him every day of his life; God was at the wheel with him wherever he was driving.

Has going to church ever taught you anything about how to get along with people or how to understand human nature? Going to any church should be a refresher course in faith. It should be a re-conditioning center where your mind gets an overhauling once a week to enable you to gain greater faith, to learn lessons in how to overcome the problems which are about to face you.

A lady some time ago told her minister that she was no longer going to attend his church; she preferred to attend my Bible class for the simple reason there was no collection taken, and it did not cost her anything. Are you that kind of Christian? Are you the kind who spends dollars during the week for entertainment but does not want to give anything to God, or to the church on Sunday? What have you ever sacrificed to God? According to the law of giving and receiving, you will get nothing back if you give nothing of yourself in service or money, or both. The more you sacrifice in this way, the

[31]

greater will be your reward. According to the Hindu teaching, this law is called Karma, and Karma means come-back; in other words, what you sow you reap, and that of course applies to giving. Ask yourself what you have sacrificed for God that you might have the things you need in life. I can as-sure you from practical experience that I did not know successful living until I learned to be a successful giver.

The New Testament to me is a book on how to gain power, how to know people, how to enjoy radiant living and how to insure myself for all Eternity, in which I am now living and in which I will still continue to live for ages after my soul leaves this physical body. From it I learned to accept the Christian Faith, the teaching of the Master in all its fullness as given by my Bible. I had to learn to master my weaknesses and my errors of thinking. When I learned to do this, I discovered the secret of human relations.

In my laboratory every day it was my job to prove certain formulae. In my religious life, I prove God often, many times a day. My religion is faith in Jesus Christ and His atonement for my past sins and sicknesses. That faith applied hour by hour with constant practice gives me freedom from sickness, teaches me how to understand human nature, gives me all the things I need in life.

I know as a scientist that the very air we breathe is full of terrific atomic energy. So I believe that God's energy is around me, at all times available to me, whenever I choose to take the good which God offers to me so freely.

Chemistry is based upon laws, laws which I can prove every day. Those laws never change. For instance, I take two parts of hydrogen and one part oxygen and I get water. No matter how many times I mix these gases in this proportion, I get the same results. Now, your religious life teaches you the same kind of laws which work for you. Once you come to believe in Christ, that through Him you can do all things, you contact that invisible power which is always flowing within you and, as that power flows through you, it brings this thing to you called life.

This faith, this contacting of God's laws is what makes sick people well, and the more you believe, the more your faith develops, the more you will come into this thing called *attunement*—attunement with God. To tune in on a radio you tune in to a broadcasting station, and the vibration tuned in to puts your instrument in harmony. Your religion as a Christian is to tune in to the source of life, which will give you a perfect broadcast, the Christ within. Your full realization of this will teach you how to understand His nature, and from that moment will come a complete understanding of human nature.

Let go, my friend, of your fears, your tensions, your worries and your anxieties, *and let God.*

THE THIRD STEP IS

Practicing
Kindness

"Be ye kind one to another, tenderhearted,
forgiving one another."—*Ephesians* 4:32.

THERE is no doubt but that this text teaches us the beautiful teaching of the Christian religion, which is love, kindness to one another, always forgiving one another. How often
do you find these qualities in the church you attend, in Christian churches? This to me is the great weakness of Christian
people today, for we find within church organizations so
much resentment and criticism and condemnation, which, of
course, is opposite to the love which Jesus Christ demonstrated so magnificently.

Human beings are very complex creatures. We are all alike
at bottom, but within our minds we are vastly different, in our
sentiments, our interests, our abilities and activities. We are
very much like a wheel, for at the hub we all have the same
basic common sentiments, but at the rim we are all different
from each other and seem far apart. We all start off at the
hub in our childhood with two simple fears, of noise and fall-

ing, but as life progresses and our experiences vary from day to day we acquire characteristics, fears and habits different from those of anyone else. Take two boys attending high school, probably born in the same social class, living close to each other, their family and other ties very much alike. Once they get through school or college with their different talents, they meet different types of people and have different experiences from day to day. These two boys grow up into young men and into mature age with entirely different likes, dislikes and temperaments.

We can classify people into certain set patterns but we have to look into the question of personalities in order to solve the problem of getting along with them. Take the case of a wife who is the dominating, aggressive type. She is usually a good talker, a gossip. But on the other hand, often her husband is a clinging vine, very retiring and completely dominated in his home life. Many active, progressive men have wives who are quiet and reserved and who very seldom take any part whatsoever in public life.

The best way to understand the differences between men is to divide them into two categories, introvert and extrovert. The former is a person who is usually shy and retiring, who likes to spend his spare time alone in study, with some favorite hobby, or just reflecting. The extrovert, we find, has many social, public and other interests. Generally speaking, musicians are introverts while successful salesmen are typical extroverts. The introvert is usually hypersensitive, easily embarrassed, writes more fluently than he speaks, does not make friends easily, worries a lot. He often spends a great deal of his time day-dreaming. He generally resents being ordered to do anything, but is very easily spurred on to do things by praise.

If he plays any game at all he is invariably a poor loser. Now the extrovert is the exact opposite. If you are learning how to get along with people, try to sense these qualities in the people you meet, then you will know exactly how to handle them, what to do and what not to do. If a man or woman is hypersensitive and easily hurt then you must be extremely careful what you say to them. You get along with the extrovert by getting him to talk about himself, about his sports and his outside interests. Be a good listener.

When you are handling an extrovert, let him talk. He will talk a blue streak about his conquests, his business, his ideas, the sports in which he is interested. He is the type who acts quickly on impulse, and very seldom worries about what happened yesterday or what is going to happen tomorrow.

Every person has some of both qualities, but those which predominate put him into one or the other class. I employed a research chemist for some years who was a typical introvert. He had a very great complex of superiority because he had a doctor's degree, and he was also extremely argumentative. He could not get along with the men at the laboratory. I finally gave him a laboratory to himself. This worked very well for a while, but eventually he looked to other fields for employment, and in fifteen years he held fifteen jobs simply because he did not learn how to adjust himself to people.

On another occasion I knew a girl stenographer who was an introvert, extremely shy, did not like meeting people, and seemed to get tongue-tied when suddenly thrust into company. She had lived for years in a room at the Y.W.C.A. She did not attend church meetings or socials of any kind, and did not meet people. In the office she did not get along with the other girls because she was hypersensitive. This was followed by a nervous breakdown. Her psychiatrist did his best to teach her how to know herself. She came to see me privately one day after her illness, telling me she was a very defeated person. I tried to show her the weaknesses in her character and got her a job in a summer hotel, where part of the day she had to meet the incoming people. She had to mix with different people after hours, and she got a new slant on living. She changed her appearance, got to be very attractive, and today she is the permanent hostess in that hotel, having married the hotel manager. However, this change did not come about until she learned how to overcome her introvert nature.

With these basic keys in your possession, you can unlock anyone's characteristics and know how to adjust yourself to those people. We all have some of both these qualities; if we were one hundred percent introvert or extrovert, we would probably be insane.

Suppose you come across a man who does not seem to like to make friends, changes his mind a great deal and is very often stubborn in his ideas. This being the case, never do anything to bring out his stubbornness, and certainly never mention the fact to him that he is unstable or that he never knows his own desires. Find out his other characteristics and keep his good qualities in mind.

I knew a man who was employed for nearly twenty years by one company. He was an introvert and there was no future for him in that company. By bringing this tendency to his attention and by teaching him how to overcome it with constant study and practice, he was able to change his personality and is now the personnel manager in the same company.

To understand people we have first of all to be kind to

them, to respect their ideas, their religious viewpoints, their sensitivities and their qualities.

Many years ago the head of a large institution and farm called me to see their calves, forty of whom were seriously ill with pneumonia resulting from a fire. The veterinary had ordered them shot, but they were very expensive and bred very carefully, which meant a great deal to that institution. We prayed about it right in the barn beside the calves, and thanked God for having begun their healing. Immediately an idea for a medication to use came to me; I followed it up in practice, and everyone of those calves was saved.

That one kindness, that one demonstration of faith in God, resulted in the company for which I worked getting orders totaling thousands of dollars, from that particular institution.

Kindness must come before all things in our daily lives. The text from your Bible which heads this chapter tells you to be kind to one another and to forgive one another. How often do we find tremendous hatreds and bigotry between our different church denominations, yes, and even between churches of the same sect. We see this exemplified day after day. This, of course, is not the fault of the churches, it is the fault of those who profess and call themselves Christians and yet are so filled with their own self-righteousness that they forget all about being kind to one another. There is a tendency to dualism in every man and woman, a tendency to good and to evil. Each of us has a little of Heaven and a little of earth in his make-up. The reason we live on this earth is to prove that Heaven is within us throughout our daily lives, so that we shall also have Heaven in the life we are to live when we leave our physical bodies.

No one ever just *finds* life worth living, because every single one of us has to *work* to make it worth living. The real proof of a Christian is his kindness to his neighbor, his relatives and his friends, under every sort of condition. This kindness works wonders over yourself, and it works wonders over everyone else; in fact, there isn't anything in life that will work so many miracles as love and kindness.

What is your relationship to your Creator, God? He is never what we picture Him as being. It is not what we think about God that counts, but what He thinks about us. How have you proved in your life your divine relationship to Him? His was the mind, the Divine Mind that created the earth, the universe, and you. You are made in His own image; your soul is the only real part of you, eternal, everlasting and indestructible, and your own mind is that part of you through which God works and by means of which you contact divine power.

Forget the old ideas you were taught ages ago of a God of wrath, a God who sent you a sickness to punish you, and demanded an eye for an eye and a tooth for a tooth. Jesus told us His Father was a God of love. He is all love, and when you show love to any person, or to an animal, you are expressing God. Our main reason for being on this earth is to express God. Everyone of us is a means by which God does His wonderful work among men. Therefore, when you are dominated by criticism or resentment or temper, you cannot express God, and you are breaking His laws; and when you break any law you have to pay the price for the breaking of that law.

Into our cities are brought power lines of very high voltage. At the outskirts of the cities there are gigantic transformers where the high voltage is stepped down to a voltage low enough for use in our homes. This is an exact example of what the Christian religion means. Jesus is the transformer of God. He is the only "somebody" no one of us has yet been able to match, this man Jesus Christ, the teacher. We must first of all believe that He came and inhabited human flesh. The Christ came down from the Father and was made man. He taught us a way of living so that we could live more abundantly, and we must try to follow that pattern not just on Sunday but every hour of our lives.

Jesus said that no man could get to the Father except by Him. When I came to a realization of what Christ could mean to me, I became a conqueror, for I got a living, vital sense of His presence which took away from me all fear of men, of evil, of disease. If, however, I make a serious mistake, if I fall into error, then I have to take the punishment that goes with the breaking of that law, and I have to realize that I have not walked with Him as I should.

You will become a revitalized person when you come to accept Jesus Christ. In our churches we usually see a cross made of brass or wood. It is not there for the purpose of adoration or worship; it is only a sign or symbol. It is usually an empty cross, a token to me of a man who died upon it two thousand years ago for my sicknesses and my sins, but who became a resurrected person. His Spirit lives within you and within me, and it is up to us to believe this. If you will do this religiously every hour of the day and practice this faith in His power within you, then you too will have a resurrection from every error, from every wrong that can come into your life.

The Christian way of life is not just sanctity; it is sanity, for you cash in on the promises of God when you learn to walk in His way of life. Your devotion to Him transcends all other

[41]

things in life. You gain a healing from sin and from sickness and develop a happy, radiant, successful personality, confident that all the details of your life, all your needs on this earth are now being taken care of by God.

I had to prove the theories of my science every day in the laboratory. In my religious work I prove God every day by prayer. You can do this too. Realize every moment that God is now waiting to operate through you, and that your mind can now open to this super-power to solve your every doubt or difficulty. All you have to do is to tune in your mind to His wave-length and all other wave-lengths will be blotted out.

How do you tune in on God's wave-length? By faith, faith that God lives, faith that God is good, and faith that all the hosts of Heaven and earth must move to an increasing purpose when attuned to His power.

You make every day a testing time for your happiness. You wake up and live in the reality that with Christ at the helm you can have life, and can have it more abundantly.

When this change comes into your life you will no longer see the evil in other people. You will see the Christ in them because kindness and love become your dominating impulses. In chemistry I learned that coal under heat and pressure becomes diamonds. The black sticky-looking tar from coal gives us aniline dyes, beautiful colors, all the colors of the rainbow. The slag refuse from this produces wonderful crystals. Mud is made into the jewels of costume jewelry.

So it is that the stresses and tribulations, the trials of your life, can produce many wonderful things for you. The hard knocks that you may have to take when you have the abundant faith of the Christ within you, will change your coal into diamonds, your sorrows and sickness into beauty. The mud of your defeats you will transform into jewels of kindness and love, because through your faith, the super-atomic power of God is at your disposal. Make this affirmation: *"I am, therefore I will, I do, I have."* Say to yourself, "I will now arise and go to my Father. Nothing can stop my progress from this day on because I believe that God is ever with me. Through this Spirit of Jesus Christ within me I am never alone and I have nothing to fear."

Let go your problem, let go your anxieties, *and let God* fill you with kindness and love.

THE FOURTH STEP IS

Getting on the Right Track ↝

"And if thy right hand offend thee, cut it
off. . . ."—*St. Matthew* 5:30.

POSSIBLY the above text has puzzled you, because it
would be a very serious thing to take it literally and to cut off
one of your hands. However, the meaning of it is quite hidden
and quite metaphysical. It means that if you have any characteristics in your nature preventing your spiritual growth, your
success in life, or which hurt other people, then you must cut
them out, you must learn how to control them and replace
them with love. Love is the predominating thing and is the
whole basis of Christian religion.

The Bible tells us that if a man says he loves God, and yet
at the same time hates his brother, he is a liar. So to understand people we must first of all start off by learning to understand ourselves, and particularly our characteristics. There is
hardly a day in our lives, hardly an hour in which we do not
think critical thoughts and say critical words of other people,
but before we criticize anyone in any way we should first of all

[45]

see that our own lives are free from error. We are so prone to see the evil in another person, but seldom do we see the wrongs in our own thoughts, our own actions and our own ways of living.

In our present day and age, more articles, more books, more "bunk," have been written about character analysis than about anything else, and for years we have known of people who make a profession of reading character by the leaves of tea located in your teacup. But it is true that if we really want to get along with people, we must practice the skill of reading their characteristics. However, it must never be simply guesswork.

Thousands of people follow astrology, phrenology, palmistry, and all these have been put to the acid test by scientific men and have been found wanting. How do you size up people? Do you think that tall men are more attractive, more dependable than short men? Have you found, or do you believe that fat men are more likable than thin men? Do you think that tall men are invariably better leaders in every profession? Have you got a conviction that the bumps on your head describe your good and bad characteristics?

The constant habits of a lifetime, the same reactions to the same conditions definitely affect your face, your body and your nervous system. The best clue to a person's character is to watch how he reacts to certain happenings in his life. Watch what he does when he is surprised, shocked, disappointed, pleased or condemned, and make a mental note of it. The constant practice of watching your friends in this way will tell you their inner thoughts.

You know very well that, when fear strikes you, you grow pale and possibly tremble. If you are sad, tears will come to your eyes. If you are happy, joy will increase your heartbeat and give you a better color. The changes you see on the faces of people are always reproduced in their inner organs. This is why the constant practice of thoughts of fear or failure will bring about physical and mental upsets. Shock very often produces the disease known as diabetes; resentment carried on over a period of years often produces forms of arthritis; while worry produces many ills such as stomach ulcers and heart diseases.

Every man and every woman should start practicing early in life the art of controlling the feelings and emotions, for emotions produce certain characteristics in the face. If you laugh a great deal, you get happy little lines at the corners of your eyes and your mouth. If you worry a lot, you get wrinkles across your brow and long deep lines down your face. If you hold feelings of inferiority, you generally shrink away from people and gradually develop rounded or stooped shoulders.

In living this life and noting thousands of people during the years of your life, you will find that by the time many people make the most out of their life, most of that life is gone. In going through life you must remember that the man to watch is the man behind the man in front of you.

When the executive of a company is interviewing a prospective employee, possibly for a sales division, he may suddenly say, "Well, what do you think you can do for us?" Very often the man becomes disconcerted, he is taken off his guard, and by the man's reaction to that question a great deal can be told of his characteristics. The executive sizes up a man very quickly by constant application of this type of psychology. He does not want a "yes" man, nor does he want a man full of his own importance.

[47]

In a school which I know of in Canada, when the boys line up each morning they are checked over by one of the masters for cleanliness, for neatness, and to see that every boy has a handkerchief in the top lefthand pocket of his coat, and one in his trousers' pocket, to see that his shoes are shined, his teeth cleaned, and his hair brushed. Boys who go to such a school very quickly get out of slovenly habits, and when those boys grow up to be men, that habit of neatness has grown so much that they cannot leave the house without going over those details which mean so much in their appearance.

Neatness in appearance always shows an orderly mind and orderly thinking. The woman who does not replace a button on her coat or who is careless about the sewing of the hem on her skirt which has come loose, the girl who does not care about the way in which her hair is dressed or whether a button is missing from her blouse, is never successful in the business world, or the social world either. Those characteristics show her mentality very plainly: sloppy, untidy, disorderly thinking. Such a person is generally undependable.

When you come across a man in your office or factory, perhaps a foreman or a boss of some kind, who has a dominating personality, you will find almost invariably that this is due to an inferiority complex. It is a part of your lessons in living to learn to study the emotions of those with whom you associate every day of your life.

Some time ago I spoke to a man taking candid photographs of people on the main street of our city, and I found out that he was most successful because he had studied people; he had read character in them. He said to me, "After you shoot pictures of the first million, you know whose photograph to

[48]

take." The people wearing smart clothes invariably bought the photographs. He never took a picture of an old man or woman, never wasted his film on a man with an old hat. He could tell from the way people wore their clothes who would be willing to pay twenty-five cents for a photograph. This man, by practical experience on the streets of a big city, was a good student of psychology, and therefore most successful in his line of work.

In this question of reading character, try to find out what pleases the men or women whom you want to understand, also what angers them, what amuses them, what frightens them and what hurts them. Many people carry poker faces all day long, but you will get beyond the poker face by studying in a very simple way their reactions to the problems they have to face day by day.

The story is told of a colored man who said to his minister that he had got religion. The minister said to him, "So you are going to lay aside sin!"

"Yes, sir," said the colored man, "I has done it already."

"Well," said the minister, "are you going to pay your debts?"

"Oh," said the colored man, "you ain't talking religion now, you is talking business."

How many of us think this way? When your business is touched in some way or other, when your business is affected by religion, do you forget all about the latter?

Religion is something we do not just practice once a week, it is something we must live in our thoughts, in our actions, every hour of the day. Not by telling people how good we are and how sinful other people are, but by the way we react in love and kindness to our fellowmen, by the way we learn to study people, saving them embarrassment, trouble and fear in any way possible.

People who call themselves Christians should be the finest folk in the world to get along with, but are they? I am afraid that thousands of Christians, members of churches and regular in their attendance, are very hard people to get along with simply because they have not learned how to find themselves.

Money, fame, position and wealth are the material things that have no reality; in fact, they do not last and are very easily lost. They seldom bring peace of mind, for many millionaires do not know harmony, peace of mind, or the happiness which every Christian should experience. To get a direct answer to prayer is the finest lesson in how to live because it teaches you how to get peace of mind, and shows you the joy of living. By adventuring daily with God, you can learn how to make a success of your life.

To know Jesus Christ, to realize that the Christ Spirit lives within you and within every person you meet, will give you a revitalized life due to the magic of believing. Your life is made by what you think every hour of the day, and just where you are in life today is due entirely to your past thinking. You are what you think.

If fear dominates your life, you reap that fear in sickness and poverty, but when you substitute faith for fear you gain dominion over all negative things, you gain success.

When you learn to believe in God in a very simple childlike way, you get the answers to your prayers; criticism and resentment never find a place in your thoughts, and you gradually come to see Christ in everyone with whom you associate. You start to radiate that personality which was in Jesus

Christ, and your positive thoughts day after day, when properly applied, are always healing thoughts.

To me, any church should be a reconditioning center where you can go to get your mind overhauled. All of us need a great deal of mental conditioning. When we get our minds renewed we live in a positive way, and life is then a very different experience indeed. Religious faith puts terrific fight into a man so that he develops resistance to defeat, to failure and to sickness. The obstacles you meet from day to day, the tribulations you have to face, all become stepping stones to happiness. Believe that God is now answering your prayers, believe that you are now receiving and, according to Jesus Christ, all things shall be added unto you. Faith without works is dead. We must act on the inspiration we receive as the direct result of positive prayer. We all need inspiration, and we get new ideas from God every hour of our day when we put our trust in Him—but we have to follow that inspiration up with perspiration—we have to work to prove our faith. Remember that the bee that hangs around the hive never gets any honey.

It is always well to remember that faith is far stronger than fear and that God is far more powerful than any supposed devil or power of evil.

A food chemist will tell you, by an analysis of a cake, the percentage of each ingredient that went into the making of that cake, and from that analysis he can duplicate the formula. Such a thing is very easy to prove in a chemical laboratory. Have you realized that it is easy for you when you start adventuring with God, to prove that He is God?

It is always easy to read a man's character when he has had a decisive experience with God, because he radiates something ıat the godless man has not got. The more you realize the raith, the power of God within you, the more easily you gain mastery over all the problems of your life.

I met a man some time ago, extremely successful in business, but completely defeated in private life. He had no faith in God, no religion; he had a very unhappy home, and his wife was at loggerheads with him. He did not drink, he had no wicked sex life, he just couldn't get along with his wife. He came to see me on the eve of a divorce action. He saw and accepted my teachings about God, and gained an answer to his prayers. He made a demonstration, he proved God. A few days later he told his wife of the change that had come into his life, but she had already seen it. She came to see me the following day, for through the change that had come to her husband she had gained a happy home, and he had gained success in his private life as well as his business life.

Possibly you think that because of your evil life God has deserted you, but God has never been absent from your life since you were born, not for one hour! He has been there with you, waiting for you to follow His rules, waiting for you to find Him, waiting for you to live up to the code of Jesus Christ. The prodigal son took his substance, and spent it on riotous living and the joys of a material life. He tried everything once. Possibly you have done the same and have imagined yourself to be away from good, away from God. But, like the prodigal son, you can come back to that Father who is all love, who is waiting to receive you this moment. He is always willing to forgive, to receive you back into His fold, into His family and to give you health, happiness and peace of mind.

Christianity is not just a way of living, it is not simply a membership in a church, it is life itself, it is vitality, it is vibrant energy. Christianity correctly practiced is a healing, throbbing, vibrant, creative energy. It is a deep therapy which can drive to the very roots of society by breaking down sins and infected centers. It will rebuild your life, mentally, physically and spiritually. It will give you the overcoming of all things. The Bible says, "In Him was Life." The life that was in Jesus Christ is also in you. In Him is creative energy, and this is the tremendous dynamic energy of life itself.

If you will start, with the reading of this chapter, on a new page of your life, if you will accept the cross of Jesus Christ as your symbol of redemption, you can be resurrected today from all the failures that have been yours. You can begin right now to take from your character the things that have made you a failure in life. You can start to practice immediately to read the character of everyone else. You can make a rediscovery of Christ.

Will you not then *let go* your past *and let God* put you on the right track. If you will do this in all sincerity right at this moment, you will feel the thrill of Jesus Christ as He touches your heart, and all things will be added unto you now and through all eternity.

THE FIFTH STEP IS

Establishing
Right Relationships ⮒

"And whosoever liveth and believeth in me
shall never die."—*St. John 11:26.*

T O BELIEVE with all your heart and soul in Jesus Christ
means that you will always get along with people. If you thoroughly believe in and live the Christ-life, you will never know
the slow death that comes from the lack of right relationship
with God and people.

As we journey through life we must learn how to get into
right relationships with other people. We must stop seeing
their defects, we must forget and forgive the wrongs they do
to us, we must show love and kindness and be really sincere
to everyone we meet.

In order to get into a right relationship with anyone, your
first idea must be to find out their special interests, their views
on religion, their pastimes, and learn to talk to them particularly about the things they like. Be sure to keep yourself free
at all times from criticism or condemnation, especially of any
other religious sect, remembering that all good roads lead to

God, and that every person on this earth has a right to worship God in the way that suits him best. Never start to discuss political or religious views with those you want to please. It is always more effective to deal with what a person does outside his working hours than whatever his vocation may be.

A good salesman tries to see his products through the eyes of his customer. He tries to think how he would react if he were the buyer instead of the seller. This is a lesson for us, for we must always try to see ourselves as others see us rather than as we see ourselves.

I have found out from experience that it is also a good idea to get the other person interested in you for some reason or other. A young lady of my acquaintance was seemingly detested by the head of her department. But one day this young lady found out that the manager was a collector of hammered brassware. The lady in question had some very fine pieces brought by her parents from India, and she took these down for her manager to see. That was the beginning of a new-found friendship. They established right relations with each other due to one common factor. I know of another case where a collection of stamps was used by a man at loggerheads with his chief, to establish common ground between them.

Are you the type of person who does a great deal of talking? Maybe you have plenty to say about nothing when you do say it. A good listener is always popular.

The most valued possession of every man and woman is sincerity. When you start to cultivate a friendship, do not use pretense, but keep confidences in the strictest manner. In establishing right relations it is always well to remember that patience, moral integrity and humility are factors that you

[56]

need very much indeed. You will probably have to learn how to swallow your pride as well as control your emotions in order to win friendships, but it is easy to do when you learn to know yourself. If you are a highly critical person, then you will find that everyone else criticizes you. If you are hypersensitive, then the sooner you stop hitting at others, the quicker you will overcome your sensitivity.

"Whosoever believeth in me shall never die" means that if you will accept Jesus Christ as your guide, your redeemer, your friend, then you have a sound basis for successful living with people of every creed and color, for in this way you have established right relations with God.

When you have a daily, yes, an hourly appointment with God, you will become so confident of His presence and guidance that you will withstand all the trials of life; you will overcome your hereditary characteristics; you will overcome sickness and you will lose your fear of death. There is no death—it is merely a passing over, a release from this physical life into a wonderful spiritual life for all eternity. When you come to believe that the Spirit of Christ lives within you, His intelligence becomes your intelligence, a source of ideas, inspiration and guidance. You lose every fear you ever had when God controls your mind, and you believe with all your heart and soul that He is mindful of your every move and is standing by to fulfill every righteous desire of your heart.

The Bible says that we must be reborn, we must be born again mentally and spiritually before we come to this wonderful understanding of God. Our thought patterns must be reborn, completely changed, and we must recognize the errors and fears of our daily lives, and make amends, and learn how to overcome these conditions which have been getting the better of us for so long. This is when we begin to find the Kingdom of God within us. Every day will become a spiritual adventure with God, enabling us to rise above every difficulty and temptation.

A Canadian Merchant Marine captain had lived a very materialistic life, but on three occasions when his ship was sinking he was saved by his prayers. Yet he still doubted God. He had laughed at any evangelistic messages he heard until he came one evening to a lecture which was meant for him. He accepted in simple faith that day the fact of what God could mean in his life. He asked His forgiveness for his sins, and he became a completely changed person. He was born again. He did not have to give up his drinking habits and other evil passions. They gave him up. He lives today a new life, for he knows that God is with him on the bridge of his ship, and his new-found faith has brought many another person to find that same Christ.

Jesus said on one occasion, "Be of good cheer," to a person whom he had healed. This means cheer up, no longer will you have a life of sickness or dismal living. By accepting Jesus Christ in all His fullness, the tendency to have a long, sad, sanctimonious face disappears. The smile of Christ radiates from your face and you are automatically cheered up even when the greatest of difficulties come across your path.

A woman came to see me some time ago filled with fears of all kinds. She had lived a lifetime of pleasure, had been a leader of society, but after thirty years it brought her the disease known as claustrophobia. I told her during her first visit the simple story of Jesus, how willing He was to forgive and forget; that in fact He was now washing her past away and she was beginning a new day if she would only surrender to

Him. She broke down with violent emotion, and at the end
of my prayer for her, her tensions were gone. She was released
immediately from all her fears. From that day on she practiced the magic of believing; she believed that her sins and
the errors of a lifetime were washed away on Calvary two
thousand years ago, and she has become a radiant personality
spending most of her time as a social worker among the
needy.

Friend, you are not alone. You are not facing life alone, you
are facing a future, an eternity with God. I do not know nor
do I ask *what* the future holds for me, but I do know *who*
holds my future. I know with an absolute faith that God will
never let anything come my way that He and I cannot handle
together. You first have to surrender, then you have to supply
the willingness and the tools, and God supplies the power.
When God actually becomes a reality in your life, anxiety
goes, but when anxiety dominates your mind, then God
goes.

The head of a girls' college, after a nervous breakdown,
came for an interview with me. She was filled with deep fears
of a past experience and she had built a wall of negativeness
between her staff, her pupils and herself. All her life she had
been a strict martinet for discipline, and she always demanded
too much of others and herself. There was no room for the
emotion called love in her life. She was a completely repressed
and defeated woman. Her psychiatrist had been unable to
help her and it was very hard for her in her first lesson to believe that God would remake her, that she could be reborn
after years of living without any faith in God.

However, she accepted my teaching of childlike faith. She
threw open the windows of her soul to Christ and an amaz-

ing change took place in her personality. The causes of her school irritations dissolved. She lost many of her inhibitions because now she looked for the good, for the Christ in her staff and in her pupils. She radiated in her voice and presence this conviction, and as the months went by she was able to establish perfect relations with all those with whom she came in contact.

What Christ did for this woman He can do for you. Are you filled with nameless fears? Are you filled with doubts and worries? Then let them go and let God take over your life. If you will let Him, He will remake your entire life and you will reap the harvest which Jesus promised, a life more abundant. The greatest thrill comes, not through sensation, but with the knowledge that a complete surrender has been made of that life to Christ. When you feel the touch of His hand, the thrill of new life will glow through you, and sickness and need will never dominate your life again. When Christ rules your life completely, all negative things fade away and you gain the health of mind and body that God expects you to have.

If we would only spend half the time in prayer that we spend in learning material ways to bring success, we would gain a thousand times the results we otherwise obtain. All my life I considered that I had established the right relations between myself and God through my church. I lived very strictly according to the letter of the law. I acknowledged my sins, but within myself I did not have a personal relationship with God, and therefore I did not know how to establish right relations with my neighbors. Then I came in simple faith to the foot of the Cross; I came to love Him with all my heart, my body and my soul. With my rebirth came my healing and, instead of fearing a God of wrath, I came to accept divine love from a Saviour who died that I might live.

The joy of triumphant living is mine today, but only so long as I live according to the teachings of the Master. Day after day we have to make conquests over temptation, day after day we must gain in a spiritual way, but at the end of each day comes the knowledge of having again *let go and let God*: thus do we reap the thrill of another day's adventure in right relations with God and men.

THE SIXTH STEP IS

Building a Name
for Yourself ~

"If any man be in Christ, he is a new creature."—*II Corinthians 5:17.*

EVERY word we say, every act we perform helps to make
or mar the impressions the world has about our doings. Courage and self-confidence make good reputations; fear, failure
and distrust unmake them.

Many people who read this book are not getting one-half
the success out of life they should, for they have not yet
learned to use the tremendous power locked up within themselves.

There are some distinct principles for building a reputation. First of all make up your mind what kind of a reputation
you would like to have. Then try to show to everyone you
meet the characteristics that will gain that end. Be consistent
every hour of the day with everyone, and under no conditions
belittle yourself, for you are a son of God.

People will talk about you every day. They will remark
that you are timid, boastful, kind, selfish, intelligent, stupid,

[63]

cheerful or sad. They will say that you are worth knowing or that you are a person to be avoided. Remember that a good reputation makes the process of getting along with others easier, and besides gains for you real rewards in the afterlife.

Shakespeare said, "The evil that men do lives after them, the good is oft interred with their bones." The good you do every day is, oh, so soon forgotten when a mistake you make becomes public. It can be held against you throughout your life. Very often the people who boast most about their Christianity are the most unwilling to forgive.

Try to get a clear picture in your mind as to the kind of man or woman you want to be: then think and act according to that mental picture. Live up to your best ideals every hour of the day. You cannot just sit still and gain a good reputation, for you must do something to build that reputation.

A good choir leader has a reputation for getting the best out of his choir; a chef in a restaurant, if successful, gains a reputation for bringing crowds into that eating place.

The story is told of a lady watching a fisherman landing a fish. "O, the poor little fish!" she cried.

"Yes," said the fisherman, "but if he had only kept his mouth shut he would not be on the end of my line."

Is this your weakness, my reader? Has your reputation been marred for life because you never know when to "keep your mouth shut"? I knew the manager of a large company who, one evening, drinking with a competitor, boasted about the sales and production of his company. That one mistake cost his firm a fortune. He didn't know how to control his tongue. Many a secretary loses her job because she talks to others about the contents of letters she has written. Knowing when to speak and when not to speak is a wonderful characteristic, and plays an important part in the reputation you are now building. Many virtues are necessary every day of our lives. We must be kind and helpful, we must be tactful if we want people to like us. Knowing when to say the right thing is a wonderful asset; but a caustic, sarcastic tongue will never reap a good reputation. Meanness means unhappiness for the one who applies it.

The housewife who keeps her home in perfect order at all times stands in good repute with her friends. The person who watches the clock in an office or factory, who just does the things he is supposed to do and no more, never gets along in life. He builds the wrong reputation, he never receives advancement.

I know a saleswoman in the dry goods department of a large store. She studied at night all she could about the manufacture and printing of linens and cottons, and became so interested that she spent one whole vacation at her own expense visiting certain mills which made the goods her company sold. She gradually became very well versed in her products. She built a reputation for wonderful and interesting service to the customers who came into that department, and became the manager of the company after a few years.

Another woman I know worked in the silverware department of a downtown store. She took a correspondence course on silverware which included the setting and arranging of tables. This resulted in her being made adviser for special luncheons and various other functions She did not have a high school education, yet today she is in charge of a huge store's department for advice on parties and catering. She built a reputation.

Every person who reads this book has talents and abilities

waiting to be used, just as these people I have cited. Your mind from day to day will be filled with ideas, but it's up to you to use them according to your faith. Generally speaking, people want to find out how much they can rely upon you, your knowledge, your wisdom; so it is wise to know your real abilities and prove you know what you are talking about. If you have no confidence in yourself, how can you expect your friends or your employer to have any confidence in you? Remember that we have no reputation at all when we are born, it is something that grows with our living. Every hour of every day in every way we are building the reputation we will have later in life.

One of the greatest weaknesses among people is inconsistency. We find people who are kind today and unkind tomorrow; who offer help to some people and turn their backs on others. We should always act in a friendly way to everyone we meet in order to prove the dependability of our character. Remember that a reputation for telling the truth is one of the finest strongholds in life, for unless we stop our first attempt at lying to get us out of trouble, by a succession of events this can lead to our destruction.

The Bible says that if a man be in Christ Jesus he is a new creature. This means that if we live the Christian religion, if we live in Christ, He lives in us. Our minds are filled with His spirit, and we talk to Him, we pray to Him until the presence of God becomes a reality to us. Old things become new. With Christ at the helm, your past reputation can be overcome and you yourself be a new creature.

Many Christians think they live up to the rules of the Ten Commandments, but how often are they filled with self-righteousness. They think that because they do not steal or lie or commit adultery that they have complied with the whole law. Yet how often do they suffer illness and disease, how often suffer poverty, because they never dream that Jesus Christ died for their sicknesses as well as their sins. This type of person often has a reputation for meanness, for lack of charity towards his neighbor, especially towards those who attend churches of a creed different from his own.

My "Lessons in Living" work has taught me that the world today is crying out for God. He has never forsaken us, but in these pagan days humanity has forsaken Him. The answer to this cry lies not in the willingness of God, but in our willingness to accept, through this thing called faith, a belief that Jesus Christ has sent His spirit to every man and woman. It is for us to recognize it and make it the greatest reality of our lives.

Today the power of God within every person is like a sleeping giant which has to be awakened by faith so that it may spring into action. How would you like to start right now to use the law of life? Would you like to prove God right at this moment as you read this book? Would you like to prove that tremendous power, His life, His love available to you at this moment, no matter how great your depression or sickness?

Then believe that you are one with God whenever you wish to be. God is a living, dynamic, vibrant force, a living reality just as available to you as electric power when you touch a switch.

Jesus Christ built for Himself the finest reputation ever held by any person who has inhabited this earth. If you will accept Him right now with faith, you can start building this moment the same reputation that was His.

When a man comes to me who is defeated in life, on the verge of bankruptcy and suicide, it is my job to teach him in simple words how to re-pattern his life, how to change his fears into faith, and how to put God first in his life, so that all things will be added unto him. No matter what your ability, the world will defeat and break you if you do not gain the consciousness of Christ and remember that when you accept Him you have then not only your own ability and power but that mystic force as well which is backed with indescribable resources.

As we go through life we may get the advice of lawyers, specialists and various experts, but if we would only remember that the one supreme authority is God, what new creatures we would become! He is the only real expert who can turn your sadness and failure into joyful, happy living. Would you not like to close this book with the assurance that no sickness will ever come to you, that your job will now work out successfully, that no one can hurt you, that no situation in your life can ever again be hopeless?

Then make up your mind to come to the Saviour, to find the Christ within you, to really let go and let God take over from this moment on. He will be the friend of a lifetime; He will never turn you down. He will start building for you now a new reputation, and He will give you proof hourly that life is not for dying, life is for living.

Do not just read these words and let them go by without trying to discover this power which I have found. Get the conviction that the Christ Spirit is within you now, that His power is your power, that His love will be directed through you to others, and you will begin to gain a reputation that will take you through eternity. *Let go* your bad reputation *and let God* build you a new one.

THE SEVENTH STEP IS

Adjusting
Your Life ⚯

"He that doeth good is of God . . ."—III
John 11.

IN OUR last chapter we spoke about the traits of character
people like to see in us. But how are they going to recognize
them, how can we bring our good traits to the attention of the
other fellow? This is an easy matter, for it is far harder to
hide your real nature than to reveal it.

People judge you by what they see and hear, and their ideas
are formed by many things: your expression, appearance,
actions, interests and motives. From these various ideas they
form a conclusion as to whether they like you or not, as to
whether you are going to be hard to get along with or not.

Try to look at all times as if you had confidence in yourself
and your own appearance. Your height or weight does not
matter, for you can get along with people whether you are
thin or fat, short or tall.

The story is told of a very tall girl who lived in New York
City. She found her tallness a bar to getting ahead in life. She

found it difficult to get boy friends, and she became very sensi-tive to her condition. Then she began designing her own clothes: hats, suits and dresses. She made them herself. Peo-ple began to look at her because, though tall, she dressed in such a way as to minimize that impression. They had something to look at now. She conceived the idea of starting a dress shop for tall women, giving such women ideas on how to dress in order to reduce emphasis on their height. Today she is the head of a million-dollar corporation, developed through overcoming a handicap of extreme height. She ad-justed herself to the other person regardless of her handi-cap.

The clothes you wear are very important, for no one can help noticing how you dress, whether you are a man or a woman. They show whether you are neat or untidy; whether you have good taste or lack it; whether you are conservative or radical. Clothing very definitely has an effect on the people you meet, so it is well never to go to extremes.

I came across a woman with a very untidy appearance: no care about her hair, safety pins instead of buttons on her coat, holes in her stockings. All of this showed untidy thinking, and when I took her to task about the matter she said that God looks at the inside, not the outside. That, of course, was the wrong way to look at it because, if she had known God, she would automatically have adjusted herself to Him, and neatness in appearance would have followed.

The expression of your face at all hours of the day is of the greatest importance; it is a true indication of what you are thinking. People with a sour expression usually have a sour and selfish disposition. People who wear a scowl give the idea that they do not like people, and a well-wrinkled forehead often shows lack of confidence, and an excess of worry. Look at your face every day in a mirror. If you are a Christian, your habitual expression must be a smile. Think joyful thoughts, because joyful thoughts give joyful lines to your face. Learn how to be alert every moment of the day, and your face will automatically have that alert expression. Feel confident about your place in life, and your face will show confidence. Every emotion you give rise to in your mind reflects itself upon your face, and the thoughts you think constantly radiate in your facial expressions. If you are a worrier, you invariably show it. If you are an optimist, you show it also, for the play of emotions is always reflected by the play of your features. You can't assume a course of action whereby your face is to show the same features to everyone you meet, for you have to adjust yourself to the particular men or women you are meeting under particular circumstances One person might be impressed by a business-like appearance, another by your gentle tolerance, and another by your sense of humor.

You have to practice adjusting yourself to the different natures of the people you are trying to get along with. A young lady with several boy friends never tries the same tactics every time; a man never uses the same tactics with every man in his office. Remember that people will try to sound out your real motives in what you say or do, for the thought behind your actions and the key to your being consistent and having people see in your appearance the right motives is to always *have* the right motives towards everyone. We like people who are helpful, we like people who appear to like us. Everyone likes everyone else he meets to appreciate him; so,

[73]

to adjust yourself to people, you have to learn to like people, to make yourself like them. This means forgetting the bad points and seeing only the good points in them.

Two men met on a train in the United States and one said to the other, "What is your occupation?"

The other replied, "I am a missionary from India, where I have converted five thousand people to Christ."

"Well," said the first man, "I lived in India for years, and never saw a Christian."

"Then what did you do in India?" said the missionary.

The man replied, "I was a government official and I used to hunt tigers. In my life I have killed scores of them."

"I never saw a tiger in the thirty years I spent in India," said the missionary.

One man was looking for tigers, and found them; the other man was looking for people he could help, and found his goal. Neither saw what the other was looking for.

It is the same with you and me; we find what we look for in people. We seem to look for the evil, to try to find a hole in the other person's armor, seeking to discredit him, refusing to see the good in others.

If we are tolerant of other people's errors and mistakes, we can expect them to be tolerant of our own mistakes, for everyone has some good qualities in him, and we must see those qualities and magnify them. The person who tries to pull down another's character is usually a Jekyll and Hyde himself, a type with many weak spots.

Every person we meet likes to feel his own importance. One of the main things to do, then, is to give him a chance to talk about himself. People like to grant favors, and it is often a good point to ask a favor of someone you want to get to like you. Most people have hobbies of some kind. Find out what they are and discuss them sensibly. People like to be asked for advice. This is often a good way to start a real friend-ship, for people like to share confidences.

I knew a man who could not get along at all with another man in his office who was a Welshman. One day he said to him, "It is very strange, but do you realize you belong to a race that has never been conquered?" This hit very hard at the heart of the Welshman, and was the beginning of a real friendship between them.

The key to adjusting yourself to any person is to act as if you liked them. Get the Boy Scout motto deep in your mind and do a good turn to someone every day, for the constant practice of this is basic Christian teaching.

"He that doeth good is of God." Do you realize that you were placed on this earth by God so that He could express Himself to men through you? For God can do nothing except through us; we are the keys on His piano. God is all good; every good deed we do, every good thought is a means for God to express through us, and this brings us to the point of seeing the Christ in everyone we meet.

We are told that Jesus Christ was a carpenter's son, yet His mission on earth was to construct a spiritual temple in the hearts of men, to teach men the spiritual laws He knew.

We are all apprentices in His workshop. Every day we work to unfold soul qualities like those expressed by the Master to make us loving, kind, forgiving, and perfect. Love is the most powerful and attractive force in the universe, and the more love you show your fellow man the more good things will be drawn into your life.

We have to know what God is before we can love Him, but

it seems strange that many so-called Christians will not believe how wonderful God and His power can be to them. First of all we must believe that Christ dwells within us; this simple belief puts us in tune with a power that will develop creative abilities in our minds.

Successful living depends upon how well you can adjust yourself to other people. The Christian Faith as taught and practiced by Jesus is the only answer.

We have today many Christian sects, the members of which often show hatred to each other, refusing to love each other, and filled with condemnation for others who practice a different Christian creed. This is all because they will not try to follow the plan of the Master, Jesus. Do you realize that Jesus spent His life going about doing good in order to express the will of His Father? Have you ever realized what tremendous love would develop in you if you made it your sole purpose to serve the good which is God by serving your neighbor? What have you done for someone during the past week, for instance? The greatest joy in life is the joy of giving. The greatest happiness in life is found by expressing love wherever you can.

If we would realize the law of love, there would be no bad relations, no bad marriages, no need to fear the rapidly rising divorce rates. The way to love is to give service wherever you can. If you have never learned to give in money or in service to God, then you have not yet learned to love God. In not trying to serve Him every day of your life, you are disobeying His rules for living, you are working against His Kingdom.

The Bible says, "Do good to them that hate you." Why? Because when you persistently do good to the people who wrong you, you eventually make those people like you.

It is well to remember that the only treasures, the only permanent treasures, we can lay up are those in the heavens of the mind; the only gold that can be trusted, that can be continually depended upon, is the gold of spirit. We are told that Jesus never owned anything; yet how rich He was in the treasure of spirit, the thing we need so much in this materialistic world.

Some religious leaders have said it is a Christian duty to be poor, but to me this is not the teaching of the Master, for He definitely said He would give you all things you might need in life if you would put love for Him and your fellow-man before everything else.

You are not a Christian simply because you follow some creed or ritual. You become a Christian only when your heart becomes centered in Christ. You may belong to a church, you may have found Christ in that church; but you may also have lost Him in the same place because you have not lived up to His teachings. Do you show love and friendship to all the members of your church, or are you filled with criticism towards some members of the congregation? Once you believe deep down in your heart, once you get into a personal relationship with God, you become centered on the Christ within and receive in return an abundance of health, happiness and harmony.

You never have to beg or coax God in order to bring His good into your life. God is like the sun; He shines on everything. It is up to you to get out of the shadows, to grow out of the basement in which your mind has lived so long. Open the windows of your soul and lift up your faith with conviction, and your life will be whatever you wish it to be.

As you close this chapter, consider your own life. Think

of the people whom you have not been able to get along with; then make up your mind to *let go* the evil you saw in those people *and let God* bring you a new vision in regard to them. Change your thinking habits and let God adjust your life.

THE EIGHTH STEP IS

Using the Force
of Ideas

"For whosoever hath, to him shall be given,
and he shall have more abundance."—*St.
Matthew 13:12*.

I T IS a well-known fact that the average man and woman
find it easier to do things according to their emotions than
by applying their reason. In our daily contacts, therefore, we
should try to keep away from arguments of any kind. Arguments create bad feeling and often result in a sense of humil-
iation.

In my life I have known many managers who seem to take
delight in making their employees feel small in front of other
people. These men are the most detested men in any organization.

You may, as a result of an argument, convince someone
against his will that you are right but, invariably, in so doing
you lose a friend. The best way not to get along with people
is to constantly try to prove that your knowledge is superior
and that you are invariably right.

Human beings love to discover things for themselves, they

like to form their own judgments. They usually resent being told what conclusions they must reach. In order to get someone you know to do something for you, plant an idea or suggestion; then train their imagination and their emotions the way you want them to go. In making a suggestion of any kind, turn a person's attention to that particular thing. The power of suggestion is stock in trade in any profession. The magician on the stage uses the power of suggestion to the nth degree in trying to make you believe the very opposite of what he is doing.

This is a story of a certain prize fight between a big man and a small man. One of the men near the ring said, "It looks like Sullivan and Corbett all over again." The little man, hearing this conversation and registering the thought in his mind, got the idea that again the little man would be beaten. This suggestion took him completely off his guard, thereby defeating him.

How often during the day do you face the negative thought that it is impossible for you to do the thing you want to do, and so are beaten from the start?

There are many people who are contrary by nature, and it is simpler to suggest to them the opposite course of action than the one you want them to follow, in which case you will nearly always win out. The medical man often uses strategy of this kind. In my own spiritual counseling I have interviewed many people who came to see me apparently on the verge of suicide. They got a definite sadistic pleasure from hurting relatives and friends and by threatening to do away with themselves, but when their bluff was called they certainly did not do any such thing.

There is the story of a daughter who had been absolutely

forbidden by her mother to keep company with a certain young man. The father, however, took the opposite tack, and told the mother to invite the young man to the house. After the visit, he praised his daughter's friend, saying what a nice chap he was. The mother was very upset and told her husband that this was a very dangerous practice, to which the father replied, "Yes, but not so dangerous as placing obstacles in her way." The mother's treatment of complete detestation for this young man would possibly have caused the girl to run away and elope with him, for she was a very determined girl; but the father, having encouraged the young man to come into the home, turned the tide, and the infatuation did not last a month, for the daughter had realized by this time that he was not at all suitable for her as a husband.

We must never laugh at the fears of other people, because often they are very real to them, and we should not attempt to remove their fears by means of argument. It is good policy to listen to their long tales of woe, then gradually submit adroit suggestions which help lead them away from their stupid obsessions.

Suggestion is the most potent of forces used by publishers, politicians, and even evangelists. Take, for example, a new book—let some book critic give a particular work a splendid write-up and you will find thousands of people flocking to buy it. The same thing applies to a movie or a stage presentation: the greater the crowds, the more people there will be to follow those crowds. We see mass suggestion at work every day of our lives.

If a man goes to the office in the morning looking pale and out of sorts, he will probably go home before noon quite ill if enough people tell him how sick he is looking. This is really

[81]

the power of suggestion. The women of our day commonly use cosmetics. This gives the suggestion of good health, and very often enables the user to feel better by means of the power of suggestion than she would otherwise have felt.

When you see a man polishing a lady's automobile, it is almost certain that this couple is engaged. When you see a woman polishing a man's car, you may be sure they are married. These are suggestions purely by appearance.

Your subconscious mind produces in your daily life evidence of the thoughts you send back to it. The constant repetition of fear, anxiety and worry thoughts will bring upon you the same thing multiplied many times over, but the constant practice of positive thinking, making affirmations hour by hour that God is now healing your fears and worries, will bring magnificent results.

How many times have you heard the phrase, "believe you can do it and you will do it"? Belief enables you to do things that were otherwise impossible, for the act of believing is the starting force which leads to accomplishment. The more you believe, the more power within comes to your aid. The practice of suggestion is used by all coaches of football, baseball, and other sports. The more the coach gives his team the conviction that they will win, the more sure is the victory for that team.

If you were faced with a sudden fright, such as meeting a ghost on a dark night, you would run with unbounded energy, for there are great reserves of strength in your subconscious mind which give superhuman strength to meet all the fears you will ever have to face.

The Mohammedan has a religion which compels him to pray five times a day; regardless of what his work may be, at prayer time he stops everything, kneels on the ground and says his prayer ritual. This gives him a great conviction that God is with him. In Haiti there is a cult of Voodoo, which is entirely a religion of mass suggestion. Dictators such as Hitler, Mussolini, Peron and Stalin owed, or owe a good deal of their success to the mass suggestion of pictures placed in every corner of their countries. Many years ago, in Canada, we would see a sign on every farm fence and barn, from coast to coast, advertising a certain baking powder. This was really mass suggestion to make people think that the only baking powder was the one mentioned in this advertisement: it was a profitable suggestion. I can assure you there is magic in the art of believing and the power of suggestion.

The story in the Bible of Jacob, and how he became so wealthy, reveals his mastery of the art of suggestion. Moses, too, was a past master at this art. If you remember, David, the small shepherd boy, killed a giant with his sling shot. Why? Because he knew he could do it.

Today on every hand we read in newspapers and magazines that the world is in for a terrific depression, that it is growing from bad to worse. When these suggestions circulate, money runs to cover, and the depression we talked about and pictured in our minds becomes manifest only because of our fears, only because men and women take part in this wrong suggestiveness.

We see also many articles written in the daily newspapers that war with Russia is inevitable. The more we talk about it being inevitable, the more we get a real fear complex and the faster we produce this war which does not need to occur at all.

There will never be another depression or war if the people

of every civilization will realize that it is their own fear thoughts, suggestion en masse, which create the ideas of these so-called hard times and international conflicts, and which sooner or later bring them into being.

Success in any walk of life is caused more by mental attitudes than by anything else; so is failure. The Roman Catholic Church places great faith in the ceremonies of the Mass. During that service certain things take place, all of which are suggestions that exert a tremendous influence over those who believe in them.

Good luck charms, sacred medals, talismans and amulets have no power of themselves. It is the magic of believing on the part of the recipient or user that makes them really effective. Alexander the Great and Napoleon were both convinced that they were superhuman individuals, and they became so because they absolutely believed this.

You can do this too.

St. Peter, we are told, at the suggestion of the Master began to walk upon the water; as long as he believed, as long as he did not see the wetness of that water, he was able to overcome a physical law.

"For whosoever hath, to him shall be given, and he shall have more abundance." This means that to him that hath faith, shall be given the truth that will make him free of every negative thing. It means that more health, more happiness, more harmony in living will be added unto him. It does not mean wealth in dollars and cents.

It does mean that if you will accept the suggestion that Jesus Christ was God and that His spirit lives within you, then by practicing His teachings, you will never doubt any more that you can overcome in the world everything negative that you can possibly have to face.

Faith depends entirely upon suggestion: the more you believe that God is now healing you of sin, sickness and poverty, the oftener you use this affirmation; the more you will become convinced of its truth and the faster you will gain the perfect answer to your prayers.

You may say, "How can I believe that I am getting better when I am still very sick?" It is never you who are sick. The soul is never ill, but the physical body in which your soul lives has from some cause or other demonstrated the sickness. When your mind becomes the dominating factor in your life, when you believe that God is now healing you and repairing the house in which you live, then the necessary change will take place.

In my counseling work I met a woman who had suffered from terrific nervous headaches for many years; she could not get relief. There were many negative things in her life, fits of temperament and resentment which she had to learn to overcome. When she came to Christ really convinced that He was now healing her, she lost the desire to do these erroneous things; she saw the Christ in her enemies, and suddenly her nervous headaches were over.

A man once visited my clinic completely discouraged and defeated because he was heavily in debt and had at the same time to find another home, which seemed impossible. He applied this magic of believing. He made affirmations every hour, thanking God for having begun to find the home he needed, but at the same time making sure that hate no longer dominated his life. In one week, the home he needed was found, and in moving from the house in which he had lived for many years he found a trunk in the basement which contained what he thought were many old worthless gold stocks. He took them down to a broker and found that they now had considerable value. He sold them and paid off his debts. The lesson to be learned from this story is that he had riches all the time in his own possession. You have those same riches available to you, for within your own consciousness right now is your future happiness, your future health and your future success.

First believe; then make use of the power of suggestion that Jesus Christ, who is now your captain and your pilot, has begun to give you strength, to give you ideas, and to give you happiness. Make this your belief, your affirmation, every hour of every day.

An artist came to see me who had had several nervous breakdowns and who was filled with fears. She had tried many different religious faiths but never gained the answer to her prayers. She attended a lecture on the magic of believing and, on asking God's forgiveness for her lack of faith in the past, she decided to rely upon the Christ within herself, and began to thank Him every hour for having begun to solve her problem.

The following morning she got out of bed with a new idea in her mind and, within four days, she had painted her first picture in many years; for her religious fears and troubles had left her. This picture showed real life, far better than her former works, and came from her new consciousness of God, from within! This was the beginning of a successful career.

Remember to look upon God as a friend. Remember also that all your life must be lived according to laws He has made. Believe that He is willing to give you now His Kingdom. Trust that He will solve every problem you have to face at this moment, if you will practice the magic of believing.

The way to get along in the world lies in the thought, the suggestion, that once you accept Christ by simply letting Him be the dominating factor in your life, and take Him at His word, believing that He is now showing you the way to a life free from error and a life more abundant, then the self-imposed prison you have lived in for so long will disappear.

Learn how to *let go* the negative suggestions of the human side of your nature, and learn how to *let God* bring happiness to you. You have the ability for successful living. You have the tools. The power you use is faith and the tools are your thoughts and ideas. Learn today how to use them, not for yourself but for God. Thus you will become a radiant, happy Christian, living in Christ and He in you, for you will have gained every righteous desire of your heart.

THE NINTH STEP IS

Discovering
Your Underlying Motives ⌒

"God so loved the world that he gave his
only begotten Son."—*St. John* 3:16.

PEOPLE give many reasons why they do things, but many
of them are only secondary, because so often they will not give
the real motives for their actions. Sometimes it is a case of
shyness; sometimes they are afraid to hurt your feelings; and
sometimes they don't want you to know certain facts about
their lives.

It is your duty, if you are learning to get along with anyone,
to find out to which emotional class he belongs; then by ap-
pealing to that dominating emotion you will win your point.

Possibly you want an increase in salary, and the boss says
you are worth it but he can't afford it. How can you find out
the real reason?

Suppose you are at the head of a Sunday School and the
attendance is dropping off. Maybe the students are not interested. How can you solve this problem and get at the real
motive?

Suppose you owned a restaurant and wished to increase your clientele, what motive can you appeal to other than reasonable prices, good food, and a clean restaurant?

To understand why people do what they do, you must be able to discover the motives which underlie their acts. You will often find that the real motive is something far removed from the act itself.

You will notice that leading men in your city often head drives for charities. They are chosen to a certain extent because of their place in the community, but chiefly because they are men who love publicity, who will do wonders and give plenty when they see their names in the headlines.

I remember a lady some time ago, whose little boy complained of a headache and could not go to school, but at eleven o'clock he got out of bed and dressed and was very anxious to get his lunch. His headache had gone. His mother discovered afterwards that he was to have had a school examination that morning which he was afraid to face. This was the real motive for his so-called headache.

Perhaps your corner drug store will offer you a more expensive product than the one you want to purchase, stating that it is much superior to the one you had in mind. But is it? In many cases the druggist gets a better profit on that article. You must always try to get at the real motive.

Many people write me from time to time in glowing terms about my work and want an interview to see me as soon as possible, but when I get down to brass tacks and discover the real motive, they usually want a position in my particular field, and at several hundred dollars a month more than they could earn anywhere else. Be very careful of the gushing person who tells you how wonderful you are and how much he appreciates you, because often this is distinct proof of his insincerity.

Sometimes people are actuated by motives of which they seem to be unaware. A lady who came for an interview one day told me that her marriage was a failure because she had discovered she did not love her husband. On discussing the pros and cons of her life in the past, I found that she did love him but that he had a superior education and wanted to mix with people of the same cultural background, among whom his wife felt inferior. Gradually through the years she felt out of place and developed an inferiority complex. Once this matter was straightened out between husband and wife, the whole situation cleared up beautifully, and they have lived happily ever since.

In solving your problems with other people, do not take only the obvious facts into consideration, for apparent reasons can be very misleading. Try to find out the hidden motives.

We often find in church organizations and clubs that friction is common among members because of different temperaments. When we hear of these frictions the real motives are not always given by either side, and we must try to find out what it could have been, and study the emotions and the conditions involved.

A man who was a very good worker with me in religious work suddenly stopped attending my meetings. When I asked him why, he said that he hadn't been going out at all in the afternoons, so I began to look for the hidden motive. Knowing his temperament, I discovered that I had given some task to another man to do, which he felt should have been given to him. He had allowed resentment to build up in his mind, and this caused him to stop attending my meetings. Once he found out that I had discovered his hidden motive, we got the matter straightened out and he became a very useful man in my work.

Possibly the plumber who comes to repair your furnace or your water coil will give you a sales talk on the use of a gas or electric heater. The real motive may be that he gets a better profit from such a sale than he would for the repair work or for replacing the old coils.

To succeed in any phase of human activity we must first of all be able to work in harmony with others, to win their friendship, their respect and their cooperation. People of every nation, every creed and every color can get along together when they have the right motives. "For God so loved the world, that he gave his only begotten Son, that whosoever believeth in him should not perish, but have everlasting life." The real motive behind the coming of Jesus Christ was not to give us a formal church in which to worship, not simply to give us a creed or a lot of dogmas or a theology, but to show us a way of living, a way to happiness, and the only way to life everlasting. Every one of us has been given special talents and abilities. We must develop mentally and spiritually every day of our lives. Jesus came as a human being to live as we do, to face the same temptations we have to face, to have the same physical make-up and the same emotions we have. He had to face the same diseases of the flesh we have, but He conquered all these. He not only conquered disease but he conquered death so that you and I could gain the Kingdom of Heaven. He sacrificed everything for you—what are you willing to sacrifice for Him?

Jesus often said that it was the Father within Him who did

the work, and He told us that this power is now within us. Marvelous, unlimited spiritual power which we can contact by means of faith, and which will bring to every person in every nation peace of mind, health joy, harmony, and everything needed for successful living. The things which have made your life unhappy in the past can be completely eliminated by conscious use of this power.

How can we contact it? By faith, by the magic of believing, by constant, hourly contact with God in prayer. Jesus taught us His relationship to the Father, and He showed us how we are all related to the Father in the same way.

We are made up of two parts, the physical part which always wants to say, "I can't," and the spiritual part which says, "I can do all things through Jesus Christ." We must learn to love God, to love Jesus Christ with a love greater than any other love and, in order to prove that love, we must follow His teachings and His life as closely as we can. Many Christians follow the teachings of Jesus Christ with the idea that God in any form is outside of men; they feel we can all call upon Him but He very seldom answers us.

To live a Christ-life is to follow Jesus' instructions, to find God's presence dwelling within us, to be filled with life, love and power—all of which are ready and willing to flow forth abundantly the moment we are willing to give up the errors in our lives and to take Him as our partner for the rest of our days.

Some time ago a man came to me in the depths of despair, entirely unable to face life. Full of fears of he knew not what, full of doubt, a complete introvert, he felt the time had come for him to end his life. He had no knowledge of God, but he learned from attending two of our lectures something of faith.

[93]

He came for an interview and he was taught how to pray. He asked God for forgiveness for his past, but what counted most was that from that moment he came to Christ. He had begun to find the Christ within him. Alcohol, and the other things which had dominated his life completely, left him. He had no desire for them whatsoever.

I advised him to pray every hour, wherever he might be, thanking God for the guidance he was now being given. At my suggestion, he also took a sales psychology course to help him to gain confidence in himself. He is now a happy, successful salesman. And he regularly keeps his hourly appointment with God, because he knows that when he began to seek for the Kingdom of God within him, he found power, he got at the real motive for living. He has *let go* his past *and let God.*

The real motive for our life on this earth is for us to express God through His Son, Jesus Christ, every day we live. God will never force us to do anything against our wills. If we want Him to do anything for us we must let Him. Jesus said that signs and wonders would follow a belief in Him, but never will God work any miracles for us until we first of all submit to His will. This is the basic, the integral part of the bargain of living.

Do you want happiness, peace of mind? Then to gain these things you must first of all be willing to sacrifice your sinful desires, your wrong emotions, your sins. Once God takes His rightful place in your heart, these things fade away; they give you up and you gain that inner peace which makes life worthwhile. It is not just a case of following Christ, of following God, it is a case of letting Christ, the perfect Son of God, be manifested in you, in all your doings.

There are many Christians who expect at some time to be

saved from sickness and trouble, but the true Christian is one who knows that he is now saved from those things by the indwelling Christ, and in faith constantly affirms this truth until it is manifest in his life.

What fears have you who read this book today? Are you afraid of your future, your health, your finances, your job? Then, in silence, when you have finished this chapter, close your eyes, hand over all these fears to God in absolute faith, and pray, believing that you are now receiving that for which you ask. Thank God for having begun to bring health and happiness into your life. This is positive prayer. It completes the circuit between you and the power called God, and the answer to such a prayer will astonish you.

Simply believing that Jesus died on a cross for you is by no means sufficient. There must be much more than this. There has to be a real change in you, a real call of some kind, a real merging of your soul with God. The healing Spirit of Christ is here today, available to every one of us, to meet all our needs, to revitalize our lives, and to regain for us the Kingdom of which Jesus spoke so often.

Won't you come to the conviction right now that you want to accept Him in simple faith? The real motive in life is for us to find the Christ in ourselves and in everyone we meet. When you make a sincere effort to find Him you will be gently led from the canyons of despair into the fertile valleys through which run the waters of everlasting life. You who seek truth, health, peace of mind—these things come only from the fountainhead—they come only from God. They come only when you learn to lean on Him in absolute faith.

Won't you get at the real motive right now as to why you are on this earth? God has a prospect in view for you, and

[95]

maybe this book will bring a consciousness to you at this moment of how changed your life can be.

Won't you try at this moment to let go everything in your life that has brought you failure and fear? Won't you really give God a chance, and let Him, let God take over the control of your life?

To *let go and let God* means a complete overcoming of the unsound motives in your life and the glorious realization of eternal happiness with Him forever and ever.

THE TENTH STEP IS

Overcoming Any Feeling
of Inferiority

"If God be for us, who can be against
us?"—*Romans 8:31*.

STRANGERS we meet from day to day are apt to take us
at face value. If we have a feeling of inferiority towards them
or towards life in general, it will very quickly show up. We
must therefore do something about it. The Bible tells us why
we should never feel inferior to anyone.

In trying to improve our position in life, in trying to adjust
ourselves to others, we should tear ourselves apart mentally
and find out if there are any such traits of inferiority in our
characters.

The cross-eyed man almost always develops an inferiority
complex because of his handicap. People who are shy or timid,
people who are weak by nature, people who have a secret
sin upon their consciences, invariably dislike meeting people
because of a sense of inferiority.

Possibly you have developed a dislike of meeting new people. Possibly you may find it difficult to remember people's

[97]

names. Hence you withdraw from the public as much as possible. You may not have had a high school or university education, and therefore cannot discuss with some people some things with which they, because of their superior education, are familiar. So you avoid such discussion.

Now whether the difficulty is real or whether it is imaginary, the results are the same. You become whatever you think. If God is with you, how can you possibly feel inferior to anyone? You have equal access to all the good that comes from God. You can demonstrate your faith in His ability to give it to you by living His life. So change your thought patterns right now. Make up your mind to beat this feeling by faith in God, and you will.

He can who thinks he can!

As we read through the pages of history we find that Julius Caesar, Napoleon and Edison, all had developed a feeling of inferiority, yet they were great men in many ways; so do not be ashamed of your inferiority complex. Do as they did, and lick it!

In our modern age we have a type of doctor known as the psychiatrist. When a patient goes to him filled with fears, anxieties and worries, he analyzes all his past life, all his past ways of thinking, and from that deduces the reasons for his present fears. He tries to outline the things he should do in order to overcome those fears.

Many years ago, I had a secretary who was filled with a sense of inferiority. The first day she arrived she told me that she couldn't possibly do my filing, and she was very much afraid of the dictation she would take from me because it would be full of technical words.

The story of this girl's life was a very interesting one. She

[98]

was the only child of two invalid parents, and all her spare time had been devoted to them because they had no other care. Her previous position had been a very depressing one with unpleasant people. Conditions at home, where there was no outlet for entertainment which most girls have, had added to her misery and caused her to become obsessed with the idea of being inferior.

However, while she was in my office she heard no negative remarks, she was given nothing but positive thoughts every day. She was taught gradually not to be afraid of technical phrases or words. She found the work extremely interesting.

Gradually she refused to accept feelings of inferiority, and month by month one could see a wonderful improvement in her personality. In five years, or thereabouts, this girl was the finest secretary I had ever known, and she left me to take a position as private secretary to a big executive. Today she is a very successful person.

Now, the people who succeed in life are those who, when they get into wrong ways of thinking, when they seem to face mountains of difficulty, refuse to accept these things. They refuse to believe that conditions, or people, or events can ever down their ambition or their spirit. They refuse to believe that any condition in life can interfere with their success. They know that nothing in life can hurt them unless they let it.

If you have had thoughts of failure, defeat and inferiority, get this idea now. Simply believe that the Bible means what it says; for when you begin to live right, when you begin to live within the laws of God, you will find that your negative tendencies are gradually overcome, because of the power within you, in which you are now trusting. This power, of course, is God.

With most people it is not the fact that they have had a failure or had a defeat which has beaten them; but it has been a holding of negative thoughts, the anticipation of failure in their own mind. They convince themselves that they are inferior to certain of their friends, their fellows or their neighbours and the longer they hold this thought the more inferior they become to everything and everybody.

One very wet and cold Monday morning in the month of March, I got into a taxi. The driver was a veteran who immediately began to rant in no uncertain terms about the vile weather. As I sat beside him on a long trip, I discovered that he was single with a good war record and that he had had two years' university training in engineering before the war, but on his return he felt that he could not complete his education, therefore he bought a taxicab and his sense of inferiority had grown to the point of obsession with him. I also discovered that he had many characteristics which go to make a good salesman, so I told him that with his background and education he should try to locate a job in engineering sales. He said this was exactly the thing he would like to do, but how could he do it?

I then quoted this text to him, "If God be for us, who can be against us?" He said he went occasionally to church with his mother but God did not mean very much to him. However, in that taxicab he came to a conviction, and before I left him I prayed with him, thanking God for having begun to find him the right job. I gave him my card and told him to come to see me when that job arrived, as I knew it would.

Ten days later he came into my office, quite a different person and radiant with happiness. It seems that the Saturday before he picked up a man to drive him to the airport. The man noticed how optimistic was this driver, who, though it was a dull morning, said it was a beautiful day. Before they got to the airport the passenger, who was a sales manager of an engineering firm, had asked the young man to come and see him when he returned. The driver did this, and was immediately placed on the staff as engineering salesman. He was just the man the sales manager had been looking for. And now after almost two years in that work he is most successful. He gained a complete overcoming of his inferiorities, was living successfully, but not until he *let* go his fears and his doubts *and let God.*

We must remember that thoughts of victory, thoughts of overcoming even small things, are the seeds from which victory springs, and you, while reading this chapter, can sow the seeds right at this moment that will give you victory over the things that have defeated you to date.

Several thousand years ago a noted philosopher known as Pythagoras said, "Man, know thyself." This simply means know your power. When you realize your own power of thought and what you can do with those thoughts to contact divine power, you can overcome every obstacle and every tribulation that may happen to you in life.

Do you realize that there is enough atomic energy in the body of every man and woman to completely destroy the whole of New York City? As this is a scientific fact, how can you have a sense of inferiority towards anything, when this power is within yourself? Similarly, there is enough power in you to withstand every sickness you ever have to face. You will overcome all your troubles by trusting this power to work for you.

You will become what you imagine yourself to be. If you

believe there is no future for you, if you believe that through certain conditions you have no chance to get anywhere, then that is actually what you will prove.

People who get ahead in life, who defeat these inferiorities, are those who refuse to accept them. These people refuse to believe in defeat, for, as I said before, it is the thought of defeat which produces defeat.

When we believe in a divine power within us, when we practice thinking thoughts of absolute faith, we realize then the meaning of spiritual victory, and learn from day to day how to deny the power of evil in our lives.

Train your mind every hour of every day to think victory and, by the magic of believing, victory will be yours every day of your life.

An inferiority complex is a disbelief in your own self, your own powers of mind. This to me is a sin, for every human being has been made in the image of God and is perfect, whole and complete. We all come across people in our lives who suffer from pride and conceit. Strangely enough, this is usually an indication of an inferiority complex, and they are using this method to hide a feeling of inadequacy. You will notice how some small, short men like to be in the forefront a great deal. They like to strut around in front of people, and when talking to you or others seem always very sure of their abilities; yet how often are they not filled within themselves with fears and doubts, depending upon this bold front to hide their inner complexes.

A certain woman complained to a newspaper in her town because her picture had not appeared in the society column. As a baby this woman had always cried for her rattle and her toys, and someone had always handed them to her. All through her life there was someone ready to do things for her; she expected to be "babied," and so developed a strong sense of inadequacy. This developed into a complete manifestation of inferiority later in life, and made her resent being left out of anything.

There is a story of two frogs. They fell into a pail of thick cream. One frog was filled with fears and inferiority, so he didn't swim around very much before he began to be choked by the cream, and drowned. Not so the other frog. He knew he was going to get out of that pail somehow, and he said to himself as he looked over his shoulder at the drowning frog, "That isn't going to happen to me!" So he placed his front feet against the pail and started to paddle for all he was worth with his back feet. In no time he had a pat of butter. As soon as he felt that solid island beneath his feet, he hopped out.

This little story illustrates in simple words the problems we all face in daily living. We go ahead with good intentions to tackle something new, but when an obstacle confronts us that we have not faced before, we often feel inferior to it, and our new proposition becomes a failure. We have to have stamina like the frog, we have to do as he did and know there must be some way of getting out of a pail of trouble.

But we have more power available to us than has the frog, for we have God power—the greatest power in the universe ready for us to use whenever we change ourselves, whenever we become converted from error into a life of radiant living.

Know yourself—change yourself.

We can all do this if we will believe that "if God be for us, who can be against us?" If you will simply believe this passage from the Bible and practice it every day, you will gradually develop tremendous faith in God, and you will find that this faith releases forces which come at once to your aid. Religious faith puts power into every man and woman to gain complete resistance to, and demonstrate a complete overcoming of, defeat.

Start now, believing that if you really trust God, if you really try to live according to His laws, you are building on a solid foundation. Every day you thus train your mind never to accept defeat, never to accept inferiority.

Has your Christianity been practical? Does your faith in religion act as a working instrument to solve the problems of your life?

I can assure you that when you constantly live in tune with God your inferiorities change into power and the impossible things of your life then become the possibles.

During my counseling work I interviewed a young lady who had made a serious mistake and had got into a great deal of trouble. The more she worried about the child she had given birth to, the more she worried about her sin, until finally she came to the point of suicide; for though she had asked God's forgiveness, she had not learned how to forgive herself. This one mistake in her life brought about a feeling in her of inferiority and fear towards everyone. She eventually came to the realization that God had forgiven all, that He had forgiven her momentary error; and she lost her inferiority complex, and later became very successful.

However, it was not until she let go her fears of what friends might think about her, it was not until she let God take over her life, that she gained this overcoming.

We are living in an age when we find on every hand apparent signs of a complete decline in orthodox religion. The world seems to have cancer of the soul and, if your religion is simply a formal one, mere attendance at church on Sunday, then it is time you did something about it. It is time you began to believe in this power called God and that He is for you in everything that is good. This being the case, how then can anything in opposition to God ever exist?

God is a very loving Father, always willing to give us the Kingdom if we will learn to know Him, if we will learn to love Him, if we will learn to believe in Him.

A lady came to me one day who had lived a very sinful, very selfish and very sophisticated life in society. Though she had plenty of money, she was most unhappy, for she had been chasing butterflies all her life which she had never been able to catch. She came to ask me to teach her how to pray, for she could not believe that God, whom she had entirely forgotten, would ever forgive her selfish life.

I told her that this was an assured fact, and we prayed believing that we were now receiving. I taught her the meaning of Calvary, and how through that Calvary some two thousand years ago the errors of her life were now blotted out. She learned how to practice in a very simple way, praying every hour of the day for one minute, in thanksgiving to God for having completely wiped out her sins. Thus she gained that thing called peace of mind. It is a pleasure to talk to her today because she carries the light of faith in her eyes, and every day of her life she experiences the joy of helping someone in need.

You have no doubt noticed that on pictures of Saints there is a halo which surrounds every holy person. Do you ever realize that every one of us is surrounded by an aura of light? This light which comes from us, which radiates from every part of our body, comes from our thoughts, and this is the part of us which attracts or repels other people. This is how you sense whether you like or whether you dislike new people whom you meet from day to day.

Remember that the whole world is run on the law of cause and effect. Every effect in your life is produced by a cause, and these causes usually are actions which come from your predominating thought processes. How careful then we should be with our thought patterns every hour of the day; because for every thought we hold predominantly in mind, we shall see the effects outpictured in life, according to this unfailing law. If we continually think thoughts of fear and inferiority, then those things will be produced throughout our lives as natural consequences or effects.

Possibly, though you are a Christian, you do not wish to give up certain wrong things in your mind: the way you handle your emotions or the way you handle your temper. If so, then by the law of cause and effect you will never know spiritual success. Happiness of a permanent variety will never be yours in this life or in the life eternal.

However, if you will from this moment begin believing in God as a tremendous source of divine energy, if you will believe that He is intensely interested in your life, and if you will believe that His laws must be adhered to, you will begin to think of God first, and yourself last. Then this Christ power within you will demonstrate every day the complete overcoming of everything that has defeated you in life. When you first come to that conviction, you are what the Bible calls "reborn," you are born again and your eternal salvation starts from that moment, for that is the moment when you start to really live.

There is an old hymn which says, "Come to the Saviour,

[106]

make no delay"; and if you are willing to believe those words, they will bring you to the fount of joy which will enable you to convert your inferiorities into success, your sickness into health, your poverty of mind into abundant living, your fears, your doubts and your sorrows into a wonderful awareness of joyful living.

Every one of us as he goes through life must die daily in a mental sense, for his negative or evil thoughts must each day die. New ideas, new thoughts, positive instead of negative, new faith must be born in us from day to day. It matters not what fears have beset you in the past, what inferiorities are now holding you back. It matters not what you have reaped in life hitherto, if you are willing today to make a new seeding time and believe that tomorrow holds promise of a harvest that will being you life more abundantly.

It is the easiest thing in the world to learn how to *let go* your sense of inferiority *and let God*; for if God is for you, what and who can be against you?

Your Code for Life ⮑

"Be ye transformed by the renewing of your
mind."—*Romans 12:2.*

IN EVERY chapter of this book I have tried to show you
how powerful is the action of thought, and I can assure you
that thoughts are things. In the last ten chapters, in particular,
I have tried to give you specific steps in victorious living that
will make those thoughts the right things.

Your whole life, your health and happiness and your success in life are entirely determined by your thoughts; whether
you think constructively or destructively, positively or negatively, you build up your thoughts and carry them through to
action every day. These actions produce results which mean
victory for you and a complete overcoming of everything
negative, or they can mean complete defeat and years of ill
health.

The power of right thinking is the power of faith, for it is
only through faith in God, absolute steadfast faith, that we
fulfill the requirements of the code for happy living.

The basic teaching of my "Lessons in Living" Bible class is that we are to see the Christ (the good) in everyone, in place of the evil. A real, lasting faith in all good things, a faith in spiritual powers, works out successfully for those who constantly and consistently hold that faith.

A lady once said to me, "I wish I had the amount of faith you possess." Every person on this earth has potentially the same amount of faith as I have; those who meet failure and defeat are those who allow their faith to be dominated and ruled by fears.

Suppose you accidentally cut your finger, you immediately place a bandage on the wound and forget about it; then a day or so later you take off the bandage and look at your healed finger. You had no doubt, you knew it would heal, so it did. But it is really God's power within you that performs that healing. Now, if through a demonstration of absolute faith like this a cut finger can be quickly healed, why not use the same absolute faith to overcome any sickness, any disease which might befall you? This same faith that healed your finger is the same faith that will solve your every problem, because it is faith in the God within you.

What kind of a person do you want to be? Have you really tried in the past to overcome your fears and your failures, to develop the personality you like so much in others? We are told by a great school of learning that out of all the people who attain successful living, only fifteen per cent have college educations; in other words, eighty-five per cent of those who develop into successful persons with attractive personalities, do so without the benefits of a university training.

Possibly as a child you were taught in your religious faith that this world was a very dreadful place in which to live. It may have been painted to you as a vale of sin, sorrow, sickness and misery; and, if you have accepted this type of religion and constantly think negatively about the world, you will produce exactly that kind of a world you have built up in these wrong mental pictures, and you will completely fail in meeting your life's problems. If, however, you acknowledge Jesus Christ as your guide, if you accept His teaching as the code upon which to base your life, then you will find this world a very wonderful place to live in and you will realize the joy of living.

Doubts, fears and sicknesses will come your way from time to time but these things will no longer trouble you for, by means of your devotion to Jesus Christ and by living His way of life, every tribulation, every sickness overcome, must prove a stepping stone to your success.

Remember well that Jesus Christ said, "I am come that they might have life, and that they might have it more abundantly." If, therefore, you have not been enjoying more abundant living, the fault is your own.

Should you ever take a trip to the Rocky Mountains, you will discover a most amazing plant, bright green in color, known as saxifrage. This plant grows on the flat faces of steep rocky slopes. You will wonder at this miracle of nature, how any plant can withstand winds and storms when it has no soil in which to anchor its roots. This plant makes its own soil for its roots; its seeds contain a strong acid which rots the rock, and by so doing it develops its own soil.

Now this is a secret for you to take note of because you can become an "overcomer" if you are willing to create from your thoughts and your everyday deeds the soil that will give you courage, faith, ideas and initiative to overcome everything which life can throw at you.

You can create miracles in your life by achieving things which others with less creative minds, and less determination and faith, say cannot be done.

Saxifrage keeps bright green at all times upon a bare rock. You too can keep your life green and thriving if you will keep your thoughts and your spirit undaunted. Never fear man or devil, for within yourself you can create the substance by which you live and rise, by which you achieve your dreams. Saxifrage adjusts itself to certain conditions, and very rigid conditions at that, but have you ever realized that all life is an adjustment? The secret of getting along with other people is in being able to adjust yourself and your temperament to the conditions under which you live and work.

Every day you must be willing to learn lessons from your weaknesses and your failures. Every one of us has God-given power within to overcome life's obstacles, but it depends entirely on the code he has chosen.

I read some time ago a statement regarding practical faith in practice which said, "To be a good Christian, we must get religion like a Methodist, experience it like a Baptist, stick to it like a Lutheran, pray it like a Presbyterian, glorify it like a Jew, be proud of it like an Episcopalian, practice it like a Christian Scientist, propagate it like a Roman Catholic, work for it like a Salvation Army lassie, enjoy it like a Holy Roller."

What is your code for living? If you belong to any particular Christian denomination do you automatically criticize other branches of the Christian church? Do you believe that only your sect has the secret of happy living? In this difficult age in which we live it is essential that we should have an undivided Christian faith. We must overcome the hundreds of divisions; we must see and know and experience Christ as He meant us to. Theology alone does not give you the essential code by which to live, but the simple teaching of the Master applied is the only way to happiness in this world and in the next.

His code is the only code to follow, and once you come to a complete conviction of what God can mean to you, once you realize that His power is available to you at all times, then that is your day of salvation, that is the day when you change your thinking pattern and make up your mind to live a new life.

I knew a chemist many years ago who had a very phlegmatic personality. He was satisfied with the small things of life but he never made headway in the company that employed him and never offered any new ideas that might be of use in his employer's business, but was content to go on in the same old routine manner.

He went to church regularly, but God did not mean much to him, until he came across a certain book that awakened in his mind the tremendous latent powers within himself. This gave him courage, and month by month as he practiced his new-found faith, God, who had now become a reality to him, brought new ideas to his mind. He gained a new and positive personality, was able to adjust himself to his employers and his fellow employees, and in a few years rose to the top of his organization.

All his life he thought he had believed in God and had fulfilled the laws of his church, but he had never made his faith in God real until he was faced with defeat. By *letting go and letting God* he demonstrated an overcoming of what

[113]

had been in his life one long series of defeats, sickness and failure.

The greatest things in life are faith and character, for these give you mastery over all things on earth. As you develop them you learn to know no fears, you begin to find that no power on earth can hurt you unless you let it. Faith and character comprise the armor you need to withstand evil temptations and wrong emotions. The person who develops a character marked by integrity, honesty and truth is the one who wins the greatest rewards in life.

Success must never be judged as the attaining of fame and fortune, for these things cannot go with you into that life everlasting to which we all must go when we have completed our training period on earth. The material things in life are very unreal for they have no permanence. The only real and lasting things throughout eternity are the spiritual values, and these, of course, come from your thoughts, your mind.

The Bible passage at the head of this chapter states that we are transformed by the renewing of our minds. This simply means the changing of your mind from a belief in fear and failure to a belief in faith and happiness, from sickness to health, from poverty to abundance, from negative to positive. You can transform your whole life by the renewing of your own mind, by the gaining of a real spiritual experience.

It is often the case that many a so-called Christian will go through life without much thought of God until he gets into serious trouble and, when there is no one to turn to for help, he invariably turns to God. We often hear the word conversion used in connection with religious meetings. To me, this word simply means the changing of your mind, the recognition that you have lived without God for so long and have reaped the natural harvest which follows such a life, and sud-denly you have a religious experience which gives you a proof of God, and in this way you make a demonstration. Whenever you see the word "demonstration" in any of my writings, you will know that it means an answer to prayer when one has prayed, believing. It is a proof that God lives, and that He is always willing to answer when we live up to His laws.

What kind of life have you lived? Are you loaded down, as you read this chapter, with problems you cannot solve? Have you lived a life of empty pleasure and sin? Have you tried to find happiness in alcohol or other materialistic pleasures of this world? Then learn to realize that none of these are real, none of them have lasting values, and none of them will bring you successful living. You must begin to practice faith in God, whom you cannot see, hear or touch, and I can assure you that this magic of believing in Him is the magic that will change your entire life.

Jesus Christ came to show us a way of life, and though He lived on this earth some two thousand years ago, He, by His life, solved our problems of today. His death took away our errors and our sins and our sicknesses, too; but when His physical body left this earth He gave us a Holy Spirit, who now lives within every one of us. And it is up to us to find the Kingdom of God within us.

When Jesus was asked where Heaven was, He did not say it was a place of pearly gates and golden streets to which we go in an afterlife. He said the Kingdom of Heaven is within us, but if we have been experiencing sickness and failure hither to, we certainly have not found that Kingdom. "Seek ye first the kingdom of God and his righteousness and all these things shall be added unto you."

[115]

The Christian Faith is so simple in its basic teachings that when you accept that faith as your code for living, and genuinely try to live up to it hour by hour and day by day, you will see all things added unto you.

When you look upon the form of a cross, do you ever think of it as the arms of the Master outstretched to you, saying twenty-four hours a day, "Come unto Me all you who are in sorrow, all you who are heavy laden with worries and fears, and I will give you rest"? This means here and now, not just eternal rest after death. Are you willing to believe that Jesus Christ is now awaiting your call, at this moment; that He wants you to follow His code, that He wants to prove to you that He lives, that He wants to give you the joy of living?

There is a statement in the Bible which says, "He was in the world and the world knew Him not," and oh, how true this statement is today—for we find even in many churches a complete lack of the living Christ. To be sure, we have plenty of theology, we see plenty of the ritual and formal type of religion. We hear about learned divines constantly arguing over set forms of church teaching and dogma but all this sort of thing of itself will never give us a way of life. It is essential that we come to Christ ourselves, believing that He will heal our sorrows and He will forgive our backsliding.

What kind of a religion have you? Is your religion a Sunday one? Do you think you alone have found the road to Heaven? If you are a member of a church, then practice the faith of that church; find the kingdom of God there and prove God through your faith every day of your life. Mere attendance at church once a week will never, in itself, give you a realization of the Christ within you.

I interviewed a lady who had suffered nervous strain for

years, and she told me she was sick and tired of praying to God. She had always prayed, if it were His will, would He please cure her, but she had never gained an answer. Subconsciously she had accepted the fact that it was not His will to cure her. So, month by month she went along still suffering this pain. However, when she was taught to pray with the conviction that it is always God's will to heal, she made a great effort to really believe that she was now receiving, and from that day she lost her nervous pain. It was no miracle, it was simply a case of what the New Testament calls knowing the truth; for, when we know the truth, it makes us free from all evils.

How anyone can believe that God, who is all love and who knows nothing else but love, sends poverty, sickness or trouble to anyone, is hard to understand. These things happen to us all from day to day, but they are never sent by a loving Father, though He allows them to exist so as to refine our characters. But He has given us a means, through the teaching of His Son, of overcoming these things.

We should realize that all the health we wish to have, all the financial needs for successful living are ours for the asking. This is what is meant by the Kingdom. "Ask and ye shall receive." You never have a care about sickness, never a fear about your position, never a doubt about being able to pay your debts, when Jesus Christ comes into your heart by means of faith and becomes a reality to you. Then you learn to love God with all your heart and with all your strength. You learn to hand over your problems and the things in life which puzzle you to Him, and thus you enter into the joy of life.

Jesus sometimes told the people He healed, to cheer up and do things! And He says to you every day, "Cheer up, children of God, live according to my pattern." Renew your mind in the pattern of God and all things shall be added unto you. The name of Jesus, what magic there is in that Holy Name! There is no other name whereby we can be saved from sin and sickness and fear. Jesus said that the things He did we can do also, and even more wonderful things shall we do in His name. Therefore, why not accept His code, and really begin to live.

You can tune in this moment on God. You can really believe and with that beginning will come the finding of the Kingdom of Heaven within.

What have you ever given to God, in service and in money? You can get nothing in this world for nothing. Before we ask God for anything, we should be prepared to make a sacrifice in service or money to Him or to our fellow men.

You cannot draw water from a pump until you first pour water into that pump, after which you get an abundant supply. You have to give to the pump first and this is the Christian code of life. You must always be ready and willing to give to God throughout your life, for, by an automatic law, whatever you give will be returned to you many times over.

The only code to live by is the code of the Saviour. It is your code and my code. Try to learn a lesson from this chapter and you will embark upon the most thrilling experience of your life; you will have begun to find the Kingdom, to create a new life for yourself. By consciously using this code of the Christ you will be what you want to be; you will learn to let go the past and to let go all anxiety.

The power you need is within yourself right now. It is not necessary to look elsewhere for the key; you, and you alone, have the key to successful living within you.

Your Guide to Happiness 〰

> "He that will love life, and see good days
> . . . let him eschew evil and do good."—
> *I Peter 3:10-11.*

HOW many people who call themselves Christian really love life? How many really love living? For centuries the Christian church seems to have taught that we live in a very sinful, very depressing, very wicked world; that there is no happiness on earth for a follower of Jesus Christ, and that the only happiness for those who follow the Master comes in an afterlife.

When these thoughts were predominant in the church, it is no wonder that we had a long Victorian era, when it was considered a sin to even smile in church or to wear bright clothes. The teachings of those days produced exactly the conditions which dominated the thoughts of the people who lived in that age.

If we hold such negative thoughts until they dominate our minds, if we look for sin and sickness in everyone, we will certainly find it.

Every day can be a blue day to you, every night just another night of misery; you produce in your daily life these very things by constantly impressing wrong ideas upon your mind. Every person living on this earth is as he is because of the pattern of his past thinking, and if your life has been unhappy up to now, then it is time for you to change your ideas and begin to practice a Christianity that will radiate happy living into your experiences.

Many of you enjoyed, no doubt, during the last summer a wonderful vacation, going to new places, seeing new areas of nature, meeting different people all living very different lives from your own. You came back with a thoroughly different picture of life from that which you had before. You came home refreshed, after being absent for some time from your daily toil, your daily worries, the people who annoyed you. Oh, how much you enjoyed the change. You lived happily during your vacation.

Was it a miserable world to you then? Did you not enjoy every minute of it? Did you not love the beauties of the sea, the forest, the countryside, the lake shore? Was it a hell on earth to you or was it a picture of God's perfection? You had a complete change of scene and peace of mind. In those few weeks you changed the pattern of your thinking, and what did you find? In the beauties of nature you found God and you found a heaven on earth. You loved life while on your vacation, didn't you? Then why is it not possible to enjoy this happy living three hundred and sixty-five days a year?

The Bible says, "He that will love life and see good days," and this tells you very definitely that the Master, Jesus Christ, knows all about life, knows all about the good in life, all about good living, and He wants you as a child of His Father, to share that good life, to be happy with Him right now.

Can you imagine the Master, Jesus, as a sad-faced, weary, miserable-looking person, a man without personality, a negative individual thinking only of the miseries of life? Would such a man have brought Lazarus back from his eternal home to continue on such an earth if it were a place of misery? It isn't common sense.

Every day in our newspapers we read about atomic weapons, atomic wars that will wipe out our present civilization, but God gives us the insight into these atomic weapons, the power of the atom, not for war but for peace. Man, however, with his selfishness and sinful nature and complete unawareness of God is able to use them for his own selfish aims, but that is not the will of God.

The people we find who are the most worried by these articles on atomic warfare are those who have never found God. The only answer to this Armageddon which we face is that the standards of our race and our age must be changed; our beliefs about God must be changed; nations must get back to God. Yes, I venture to say that the so-called churches of God must get back to the simple teachings of the Master.

No United Nations, no meetings at Lake Success can ever be the means of changing this world into a world of peace; first we must change the lives of individuals. We must begin to think rightly, to live rightly, according to the laws of God, and peace will follow.

Everyone, regardless of his age, can completely change himself, and this change will help to change those with whom he associates. Our happiness and the happiness of our relatives and neighbors depends upon every one of us. Once we find the Christ within, we radiate that light to others, and can change our home life, our occupational life, our community life and, eventually, the life of the nations.

A member of Canada's Parliament wrote to me some time ago about his completely changed viewpoint on Christian living, since applying the teachings of my book, *Lessons in Living* to his daily life. This book showed him what a selfish individual he had been all his life, and through his new conviction he gained the overcoming of a disease. Now he puts God first in his life and his politics.

A mother told me of how she had come to a complete restoration of her faith and religious convictions through the study of my writings. Oh yes, she had been a regular churchgoer, but at home she lived in constant fear of sickness for herself and her children. She had adopted a very nagging habit toward everyone, for she suffered constantly from nervous prostration, and at night was too tired to go out with her husband. What a difference in her life and her home since she began to practice the teachings set forth by our Lord. The children can now have their friends visit them in their home; the mother does not mind the upset they make. She has given up the constant irritations that occurred every day in her life. She had thought that her duty to God was simply to go to church every week. Now she finds the Master with her in the kitchen, at the washtub, or wherever she may be occupied. Of course, all this needed perseverance and constant practice, but she has now found the guide to happiness.

You too can find this nearness of the power within yourself. You must come to the realization that it is a very happy and practical thing to be a Christian and to radiate happiness and health every day of your life.

Many years ago I met an old lady of eighty-six who lived in a small thatched-roof cottage in Ireland, and every day of her life had to descend a five-hundred-foot cliff by a narrow path. She raked the seaweed after the tide went out, dried it, then burned it and carried the ashes to the top of the cliff. These were sold to a factory which gave her about twenty-five cents a week; she paid eight cents a week for her house and, radiantly, she told me how happy she was and how good God had been to her. One of the sons raised in this tiny cottage won the Victoria Cross in the First World War.

What about you? Could you be happy for blessings untold under such conditions? You can make your life a happy one if first of all you will forget and forgive the past, if you will learn to live one day at a time, believing that a radiant future is yours.

Fears and diseases will follow you no more when you learn from the depths of your heart how to let go the evils of your life and let God take care of you.

There is a simple technique for living the Christian life. First of all you must believe in and accept the teachings of the Master. You must read about Him every day in the Gospels. You must make an appointment with Him every day to talk to Him. Through this simple faith you will demonstrate a life of overflowing abundance and overwhelming happiness. You will learn how to put yourself last in your life, and your fellow-men before yourself. You will then have a most powerful mental attitude towards life. This is faith, and the Bible is full of stories of what faith has done for others and what faith in a living vibrant Christ will do for you. Nothing in this world will be impossible to you.

What about the promise, "What things soever ye desire, when ye pray, believe that ye receive them, and ye shall have them"? What a marvelous promise this is, and how true you can prove it to be.

Stanley Jones says that it is much more fun being a Christian than going to the devil; one feeds a life, the other satisfies an impulse. One ends in a mess, the other in the joy of living.

Many things will happen to you when you take Jesus Christ as your guide to happiness. Many little coincidences will take place in your daily life which you had previously looked upon as good luck. But they are all part of that divine plan, for the world is created by a God who runs it on laws, and when you live up to those laws, then you *let go and let God*. The joy of living becomes a daily coincidence with you.

A lady leaving my Bible class one Sunday afternoon was so uplifted by my message that she put everything she had into the love offering box, and when she got into the bus she had no money or bus tickets, and had to ask her friend to pay her fare because she had given all she had. "Well," said her friend, "Dr. Cliffe tells us that when we give one ticket two come back to us." As they got off the bus, lying on the road in front of them were two tickets. Yes, you say, but this was mere coincidence, just good luck. Oh, no. God looks after the little things and the big things when you really learn what it is to know Him.

A business man came to see me some time ago who had failed in business. While he seemed to have good ideas, he did not have enough working capital. After discussing his life with me, we discovered he was filled with criticism and resentment of former employers and his life was dominated by these resentments. He had to ask forgiveness of his employers. He had to ask forgiveness of God. He had to seek peace and follow it; he had to surrender his life to Christ. Then he gained his answer. Several offers of capital came to him from sources he had never known before, and the more he practiced living one day at a time, the more he forgot that wicked past, and the more successful he became.

Do you believe that God wants you to live a miserable life? Do you believe that He wants you to have worries, anxieties and sicknesses? That is not the teaching of the New Testament. The way I interpret it, He wants you to be happy and to radiate that happiness.

Many people want to be happy but do not know how. They take their happiness from the material things of life; but do you often see happy faces leaving a movie or cocktail bar? Not really happy faces.

Then we have that type of Christian so proud to tell you how long he has been saved, who thinks it a crime to smile in church. I often wonder why so many Christians frown so much in their daily lives and in their jobs. They don't realize that it takes twenty-seven face muscles to form a frown, and only eight to make a smile. This kind of Christian naturally overworks his face.

The teachings of Jesus make us happy, radiant, joyful, successful. Jesus makes you glad; He makes you sing. Do you learn how to prove Christ in your church? Does going to church make Christ a reality to you? The finest cathedral in the world is only a pile of stone if we do not learn how to find the Christ there, if we do not learn lessons in living in that cathedral which will be a guide to happiness for you and me.

Your guide to happiness is the Christ—His way of life.

Do you want it? There is a price to be paid. You must surrender your whole self to God through Jesus Christ. Pray for it, act on it, believe it, and you will begin at once to feel His power in you. Plant this idea firmly in your mind, affirm it every day, strive for it. Try to make yourself worthy of being a temple for His Spirit.

Bury your sins without doubt or fear, and your fondest dreams for happiness will come true. There is not a soul upon earth who cannot make his or her life a marvelous thing, a tremendous experience.

Let go those things in life which have kept you from happiness, *and let God.*

There Is Magic
in Believing ⟐

"If thou canst believe, all things are possible
to him that believeth."—*St. Mark 9:23.*

As YOU go through life you will find that people in general are more interested in themselves, their own health, their own success, than in anything else.

The Bible says that any Christian can achieve any good thing if he is willing to believe strongly enough in it. This is a force, a factor which few Christians seem to realize and, not realizing it, they do not use it to achieve happiness and success.

There are many leaders in the world who have reached the top of the ladder because they have found this source within them and, having discovered it, use it from day to day. The science of right thinking is as old as man, for the Bible says, "As a man thinketh, so is he." If you have not been able to succeed in life in some particular way, then that tells me at once you are lacking in belief, you have not yet realized the power of the Man inside you, the Christ within. If you are willing to believe in this power which you cannot see, feel or touch, and practice that faith every hour of the day, then all things will become possible to you.

In our everyday lives we see so many people interested only in those things which must be left behind when the soul passes on to eternity. It is most regrettable that in churches of every denomination we find people who are not interested in the study of spiritual matters, particularly as they apply to daily living.

There is genuine magic in believing for every one of us. If you constantly think about past failures, if you allow past sins to bother you, if you hold resentment against someone who has wronged you, then you have no faith, then you become a failure.

Some years ago a lady in this city who had studied the magic of believing for several years was left a widow. After the funeral expenses were paid, she had a credit balance of twenty-nine dollars in the bank. In these intervening years she has become a very successful business woman and now owns outright her own hotel, worth over a hundred thousand dollars. She proved her magical faith.

Many of us are filled with the idea that, because we read our Bibles each day and say routine prayers and attend church once a week, that we are the only real Christians. This sort of worship is often based on a faith that goes no further than the lips, whereas real service to Almighty God has to come from a conviction, right from the heart.

A woman came to see me several months ago suffering from a nervous rash which a dermatologist had been unable to heal. On discussing her problems we discovered what was wrong with her thinking. She gave up that wrong to Christ, and her rash disappeared in twenty-four hours. It has never returned. Her constant fear was of something that had happened years ago; this fear caused the rash. The moment she gained faith in God, through the magic of believing, her "incurable" condition disappeared.

In hospitals today, every recovery from a serious operation depends on this faith, and the person who will not release his or her fears after an operation will make no recovery at all.

Are you afraid of certain things happening to you? Are you afraid that some disease is in store for you, or that later in life you will be left without means to support yourself? Then these things will happen just as you plan them in your own mind, because you are using wrongly your power of believing, you are placing your faith in wrong thoughts, in evil thoughts, instead of the good which God expects of you. We produce in our lives whatever we think, whatever we fear. A beautiful building, beautiful clothes, any work of art, a radio, a steamship, an airplane—all had their origins in thought, in the minds of men. No empire, no fortune was ever built without thought. Yet have you ever realized that your thinking patterns today can make you successful or bring you complete failure?

In many universities today the power of thought transference is being studied. It has been definitely proved that thoughts are things. Every thought you think goes out from your mind on an electrical impulse, on an ultra short wave, and it is possible to train people to be receptive to thoughts.

What are you willing to sacrifice from your present ways of living in order to make your dreams come true? Are you the type of person who feels that if he sits in a draft he will get a cold? Do you think if you go out on a wet day without your rubbers you will get the flu? You surely will, because of your wrong mental pictures, using the magic of believing for the wrong things. You need never have a cold at any time. Why should a little bug that you can't even see under a microscope be capable of dominating your blood stream, your body? Why should you be afraid of some dust from a flower which results in giving you two months of hay fever each year?

The moment you make up your mind to overcome your fears, the moment you really practice the magic of believing in this power within you, you will never demonstrate or produce any of these ills in your physical body again.

We hear a great deal about the science of hypnotism, and it is very easy for a psychiatrist to demonstrate to you or to anyone how your subconscious mind believes everything it is told. I have on many occasions seen a psychiatrist hypnotize a person, attach to his hand a postage stamp, and then tell the person this was a super mustard plaster that would blister his hand in three minutes. After exactly three minutes had elapsed the victim would scream with pain, and in each case a blister covering the same area as the postage stamp was produced.

We should all learn how to make positive statements, positive affirmations, every day in our lives. As we leave our homes in the morning we should say to ourselves, "Underneath me are Thine everlasting arms." And with that conviction will come complete freedom from fear of anything evil that might assail you. Such positive assertions, faithfully repeated, will build up in you the power of believing that God is now protecting you, that God is now doing wonders for you to bring you into happy living.

On the other hand, of course, repeatedly denying God's ever-present help, will gradually wear down your resistance to evil things, because you have built up the evil in your mind instead of your God power. For instance, tomatoes were once believed to be poison, and many people actually died through eating tomatoes, because they put their magic of believing to work in the wrong direction.

I often wonder why so many Christians look on the dark side of life, fearing the future, fearing death, and fearing life itself. This world was made by God for our happiness, for our happy living, and it is only man's negative thoughts, man's selfishness which have produced the very things he fears. No follower of Christ need ever suffer sickness or poverty, need ever be without any good thing which he needs, and all that is required is to follow the principles of the Master and practice the magic of believing in God, every hour of every day.

Have you ever realized that when you hear an unsavory story about some public figure and, whether or not you know it to be true, you accept it and so condemn that person, you are forgetting all the good things he has done. This does not hurt the man in question but, through wrong use of your belief, through wrong mental pictures, you will produce failure and sickness in your own life.

As a chemist I have faith in science, and I can prove it every day. The salt we use so commonly is made up of two deadly poisons; combined in a certain manner they produce a commodity which is absolutely essential for every one of us. This is the magic of believing the laws of chemistry.

Christian faith is the greatest spur to success. Take the case of the Maid of Orleans. She had a dream early in life which made her believe she would be the leader of her country. She gave her life to prove an ideal. Her firm belief in God's will led the armies of France to rid that country of its today this simple maid is revered as a Saint.

oy is very young he lives in a world of imagina-
's cowboys and Indians and, as he plays, really believes that he is a cowboy or an Indian. A little girl as she plays with her dolls lives in a real fairyland, really believes during her hours of play that she is a mother—and look at the happiness our children get from practicing such beliefs. Jesus said that we could not enter the Kingdom of Heaven unless we had the faith of a little child. Only by the magic of believing in Him will we find the Kingdom of Heaven within ourselves.

Have you ever thought that you probably produced your present insecure position in life through believing in the wrong things? Maybe you loved to let your temper go, maybe you have on many occasions lost control of your emotions. Maybe you thought it the right idea to be modern and to ridicule the old-fashioned ways of your parents. These are all wrong mental attitudes, and will produce in years to come the equivalents of your wrong mental pictures, in suffering and defeat.

The basis of all healing is faith. In order to recover from sickness a person must have faith in his doctor, his surgeon, his nurse, and the medicines which are given him, for without this faith the patient would never recover. How many times have you not seen a patient go down hill rapidly when his doctor told him there was no hope of his recovery?

Once I was asked by a medical doctor to visit his wife, who had suffered two strokes, was partially paralyzed, and whose blood pressure was so high that she was in imminent danger of a third stroke. This woman listened to what I had to say, and so complete became her conviction and faith that in two days she got out of bed, took a bath and did her own hair.

When all human means had failed, the power of the magic of believing in Jesus Christ destroyed her fears and brought healing to her physical body.

When you learn to swim, to ski, or to ride a bicycle, you are using this thing called faith, believing you can do these things. It is just as easy to fasten your imagination and belief upon God, who is willing to work wonders for you if you will let Him.

Think of God as a wonderful Father, and picture yourself every day as a happy, healthful person; then make it come true by the constant hourly practice of tuning in on God through faith, handing over your problems to Him and you will reap that abundant life which Jesus came to bring.

I am no theologian and I have no desire to study orthodox theology in any university. I simply believe that God is my Father and that I am His son and that my mind is a part of His divine mind—and by this magic of believing I can be in tune with that tremendous mind of His at any time I choose and, by so doing and by so believing, I can gain the answer to any problem which I have to face.

I believe with all my heart that Jesus Christ is divine and that He came to show me a new way of living, a new way of loving. When I came to Him, giving Him my heart; when I placed Him first in my life; when I told Him it wasn't what I wanted to do but what He wanted me to do; then this communion with God brought me release from all my past errors.

This communion with God many times a day is simply communion or fellowship with the principle of life. This is what gives us ideas and brings peace and harmony in our lives.

In the New Testament, St. Paul says that those who took the sacrament of the Lord's supper unworthily, without thinking about it, suffered from diseases and poverty, and died. But if we are willing to come with a pure heart, with simple faith, then, through the elements of bread and wine, we receive, in a spiritual way, power to overcome all things. We make a communion of fellowship with God and with our loved ones, and we take His power, which comes to us by faith, to enable us to withstand the perils of life.

What you get out of religion is entirely up to you. You can make your faith a super atomic dynamo or you can make it a routine affair without progress. You can be healed right now and your healing can start at any time regardless of how serious your condition may appear to you, if you will let go your fears and give God His rightful place in your life.

How can you afford to refuse this man, Jesus Christ, when you see every day in your life what faith in Him can produce? This Christ became a reality to me many years ago; and the freedom from pain, from sickness and from fear which I have had in these intervening years is what I am trying to offer you through the medium of these words today. What He has done for me, what He has given me, He is willing to give you, if you will try to practice the magic of faith, the magic of believing.

Yesterday Ended
Last Night 🪶

"Seek ye first the kingdom of God, and his
righteousness."—*St. Matthew* 6:33.

W HAT do you desire most from life? If it is good then
the Bible says that you can have it. It says that if you seek first
the Kingdom of God, all things shall be added unto you:
peace of mind, freedom from worry, the best of health, all
your material needs including food and clothing.

Many people feel they cannot have successful living without trying to live the life of a saint, without being saints
themselves. The Bible does not say that you have to be perfect as Jesus Christ, but it does say that you must seek His
Kingdom first of all. Try to find God by devoted living.

I do not believe for one moment that saintliness is the
answer to this question. It is righteousness. The ancient Greek
meaning of righteousness is the dictatorship of the kingdom
within. In other words, let your life be dominated by God,
let go of evil emotions. Let go of wicked tempers and evil
things. Believe that His creative Spirit within you is now

working for you, and His Spirit within your mind will work out and solve your problems in life. *Let go and let God.*

Only by daily contact with God, thanking Him ahead of time for the things He is going to make possible in your life, will you gain abundant living. Jesus Christ used and taught this method. It's up to you to follow His teaching.

If we look in the Old Testament, we find that David thanked God and praised God with his Psalms, particularly when he was in trouble. Daniel thanked and praised God when he was in the den of lions. St. Paul, we are told, sang hymns and praised God when he was in prison and, as a result, God opened the doors of that prison and let him out.

Wherever we look today, we see people living in prisons of their own thinking. Many people go on suffering day after day through constantly thinking of their past evil living. Many of them are held fast by that devil called alcohol, which they still continue to drink knowing full well that each additional drink brings them into a greater prison than ever before. These people have never learned how to turn their thoughts to God, which is the only way to gain release from this downward pull. They do not believe that their bodies are temples of His Holy Spirit.

How many people are held day by day in the prison of a bad temper? It is all very well, when your evil tongue has spent itself and you are exhausted, to say the devil tempted you. No devil, no satan, tempted you at all. You are passing the buck to some being you have never seen, instead of taking the blame upon yourself for allowing your temper to hold you in bondage.

How many people today are living in sorrow and sickness because of their resentments towards people and conditions

[136]

that brought misery to them in past years. They will not let go the memory of a past that is dead.

So many Christians let little things, the non-essentials in life, disturb their peace of mind. For instance, one lady who attended my lectures in Toronto refused to sit in the church. She preferred the Sunday School, because she said she did not like to see me dressed up in my vestments. She will wonder why her prayers are not answered, yet she will no doubt stubbornly refuse to remove this "grit" which is blocking her channels and wearing down her bearings.

Maybe you have failed, in your journey through life, to find life really worth living. Maybe you have married the wrong man or woman. Maybe you have gotten into debt and feel that your life is an utter failure.

No man on earth has ever failed in life so long as he retained his faith in God, so long as, day by day, he sought the Kingdom of Heaven.

Throughout the years I have been engaged in spiritual work, I have found that most people need a lesson in living in such a way as to forget the past. It is not easy to forget the memory of someone who has deliberately hurt us, who has done us a great deal of damage materially. It is never easy to forget, but unless we are willing to forget and forgive as Jesus did, how can we expect God to forgive us our errors of thinking day after day?

I had to begin seeking that Kingdom within myself and, once I found it, by constant faith, by constant hourly practice of turning to Him, I gradually gained a greater consciousness of the powers available to me and to you every single second of every day and night.

I had to learn first and foremost that all my yesterdays

[137]

ended last night. There is no yesterday to remember, there is no future to worry over; it is only *today* that exists, and we all make history for ourselves each day we live. The day we make the decision to put God first in matters great or small, that definitely is our day of salvation.

Then no enemy can invade your heart, no alcohol or emotional reflex can ever dominate your life, when you trust that power of God which is within your soul. Please believe me when I say, right at this moment, that all your yesterdays with their records of failure, resentments and hatreds ended last night.

No longer need you live in fear of that past, no longer need you fear the sicknesses you suffered in that past life, if you will only put the past behind you and live for today. If you refuse to do this, then your life will be a failure, not only as long as you live in the physical world which we know, but in that life which is to come.

Some time ago I met a woman who had an epileptic daughter, one who had suffered from this disease from birth. Previous to the birth of this child, the mother had fallen into a certain type of sin, and, from the birth of this baby, she was filled with tremendous fears, believing that God had sent hei an epileptic child as punishment for her sin. Naturally, under these conditions, the child made no headway whatsoever and it was essential in this case, as in many others, to heal the mother first. She had to be taught that she had been forgiven long ago and she had to learn how to forgive herself.

I explained to her that God did not want this sin brought up from day to day in her consciousness when He had already forgiven her many years before.

How the child came to be an epileptic is not for us to know.

[138]

I explained to the mother that it was sufficient to know that God's grace was enough to heal that child and, if she would come to a complete surrender of her past fears and let go that past and let God take over, then not only would she be healed but the daughter would also recover.

This is exactly what happened. From that day to this, that child has never had an attack of the disease.

A great man said some time ago, "Duty and today are ours. The results of the future belong to God." Have you ever realized that there is not any limit to the question of God's goodness to you as His child? Have you ever realized that you are deliberately limiting God's goodness when you are not willing to forget your past? No matter what you may think about hereditary conditions that have come down to you, no matter what you think about your past existence and its evils, God can and will redeem it and give you perfect understanding of your relationship to Him.

When we start to practice the teachings of the Master, every trouble we have to face, every experience of failure in our past life and present, becomes a stepping stone to successful living with Christ. Every trial is a spur to greater success and a greater future than we have ever known.

Many years ago the cotton industry in the United States was almost blotted out by a bug called the boll weevil. When this happened, did the planters get scared and run away from the country? No, they began to fight with every weapon of science available to them, and they licked it completely. It is now only a memory in that area.

May I ask you, as you read this book, what boll weevil, what bug, what fear is now sapping you? Do you think because your parents died from some organic disease that there is no health in you and that you will inherit that disease? Have you been told already that there is no hope for you as far as your bodily health is concerned? Then, if so, a fear bug has got you within its grasp and, if you continue in this way of thinking, this fear bug will master your life. You should remember that the things that are impossible to man are always possible to your Father, God.

A short time ago I received a letter from a woman in a coastal city, thanking us for the marvelous healing that had taken place in her son, incarcerated for several years in an insane asylum. She had written for my literature and requested my Bible class prayers. She was taught to pray positively, believing that she was now receiving. She was taught not to look back into the past, that God had already forgiven that past in the boy's life and had begun his healing, although he himself knew nothing about what was being done for him.

She was no more a saint than any one of us. She was no closer to God than any one of us, but she let go her fears of insanity, she let go her yesterdays, and in a very short time her boy's mind came back to normal and he returned home happy and sane.

A man attended my Bible class a few Sundays ago and told me that he had come from a distant city six months before for treatment in one of our hospitals; his condition was chronic neuritis of the legs. He could not walk at all and he was being sent home as incurable when, the Sunday before, he heard a sermon given by me on the subject, "Healed by a Touch." This sermon came to him in the hospital by radio and as the sermon ended, he said he put forth his hands from the bed and said, "Jesus Christ, I am touching the hem of

[140]

your garment. Now my healing has begun." One hour later he discovered that he could bend his knees in bed, he got out of bed and found he could walk. After one week he was able to come to the Bible class before he left for home without the aid of crutches or a cane.

He was a Christian man but had never come into such a consciousness of God until on that Sunday morning in his hospital bed he suddenly let go his fears and God took them away.

When you begin to practice every hour of the day a consciousness of God, you get this thing called righteousness. When you learn to thank God for the lessons of your past life and realize that all your yesterdays ended last night, then the worries of those yesterdays no longer have any hold upon you at all. The same blessed assurance that "Jesus is mine," that Jesus is in you, that you have accepted Him, that you have found Him, that you will live with Him forever and forever, becomes a daily, hourly conviction and you know you will never let Him go.

Our physical bodies can be placed in prison but no one can ever imprison a thought. No one can ever cage up an adventurous spirit, and this is what makes human beings different from animals. This is what the Bible means when it says, "For as many as are led by the *Spirit of God*, they are the sons of God." Would you not like to feel that you were a son of God? that you have for your Father the greatest power in the universe? that you will never again feel alone in this world? When this conviction comes to you, when you realize that Jesus Christ suffered tortures and death for you, your sicknesses and your sins, then you will have an urgent desire to put Him first in your life.

No longer will you say, at any time, that it cannot be done. It can be done if you say it can. So get wise to the reason for your failures. Ask forgiveness for your past and pray right at this moment, thanking God for having begun a new life for you today.

The Bible tells us that there is but one power in life. So forget the devil and all his works. Deny his mythical ability to hurt you. Throw him out of your heart and mind. Believe that you can do all things through Jesus Christ who strengtheneth you. You will then learn that life is for living, happy living, radiant living.

All your yesterdays ended last night. Today you start adventuring with God; so plan to begin the finding of that Kingdom of Heaven within you right now. Find His righteousness, and you will learn the secret of how to *let go* the failures and evils of your life *and let God.*

The Ten Commandments
—and You

IN THE course of my work I have found it to be quite common for people to have the idea that they strictly live up to the Ten Commandments so long as they are not conscious of deliberately breaking any one of them.

Such people do not lie or steal or commit adultery, but they seldom realize that there are many, many sins not listed in the actual words of these commandments that are definitely in the same category.

Let us take the first commandment, "Thou shalt have no other gods before me." To the great majority of Christians this means we must not worship any pagan gods like Mohammed, Buddha, Confucius or a thousand other gods. But the metaphysical or spiritual interpretation of this commandment, as it is worded, does not mean just that particular idea.

Of course no Christian would worship a statue, a crucifix,

a religious relic, or any of the pagan gods; but when we put pride, resentment, criticism, condemnation or hatred first in our lives, when we constantly think and act upon these thoughts, we are placing these things before God. In this way we deliberately break the first commandment and, in so doing, we have to suffer the punishment that goes with it. God never punishes us; when we do wrong we punish ourselves because in holding wrong thoughts, in performing wrong deeds, we, of our own free will, disobey God's teachings.

Likewise, the man or woman who puts money, social position or other forms of false security before God is breaking this first law every day.

The average Christian would not like to be accused of bearing false witness, but do not many of us repeat idle gossip without proving the accuracy of our statements? And how many people mar their happiness by coveting other people's possessions, their success in life, their health, their positive attitude towards life, instead of going direct to their own Father in simple faith for these riches of the Kingdom which He is waiting to pour out upon them to fulfill every righteous desire of their hearts.

I cannot conceive of a single person who could truthfully say he never breaks any of the Ten Commandments. In attempting to break them we break ourselves, for God's laws are immutable.

It is well therefore for all of us to discover ourselves, to find out how in a thousand little ways we have tried to break some of God's laws, maybe are trying to break them now. Let us then root them out, do something about overcoming these evil characteristics, and in so doing we will learn how to *let go* and *let God*'s laws work for us.

[144]

The Law
of Cause and Effect ↝

"And the fruit tree yielding fruit after his kind."—*Genesis 1:11.*

ONE of the most important lessons we learn from the Bible is that everything in nature, everything in life, everything in mind, produces after its own kind. Trees, plants, vegetables, the animal kingdom, all produce according to their own classification and the farmer knows only too well that whatever he sows in his fields, that only will he reap; he never expects anything else.

As we look through the Bible, we find the story of Elisha and the widow who had just a little oil, yet when Elisha blessed it, he brought unlimited wealth to her, not in money, but in oil, after its kind.

When the crowds had no food to eat, Jesus took a few loaves and fishes. He fed thousands with them and there was an overflow of food. He produced bread and fishes, after their kind.

So it is with us, every hour we live: whatever we think,

whatever we allow to dominate our minds, so we produce in our physical bodies. If we persist in thinking fear and poverty, then, unfortunately, these things we will reap according to law. By that same law, thoughts of health and abundance will produce after their kind and our lives will show forth these blessings.

Possibly you have met a person who often says, "I can't afford to give. I am too poor to give anything to anyone." This person has built up a very negative idea of substance and through the years of his or her life that person will never have anything to give, because he will never receive.

Our abilities and talents, the skills we possess, are all forms of power and, if we want to increase our stocks of these things, we must put them to work. We must have faith in them by thinking success thoughts, thinking health, thinking happiness, thinking victory.

We are told in the New Testament of a man who gave talents of silver to his servants. One of the men was so afraid of losing this money that he buried it in the ground. For his lack of foresight and lack of faith, he was discharged from his job.

Every man and every woman has talent and ability along certain lines, but oh, so many people have long since buried their talents. We heard a lecture in our parish hall which was an inspiration to all those who heard it. The lecturer had the ability to write, to lecture and to paint, but she only had these abilities because from childhood she had used the talents which God had given to her.

Some time ago the general manager of a large business, whom I did not know, met me downtown and told me of one of his employees, a lady who had been with him many years.

She had great ability, it seems, for organization but she ruined things completely by the lack of control over her temper. She didn't develop her talents as she should have done, and, because of her disposition, she was very much disliked by her co-workers.

However, it appeared she began attending a course of my lectures on "Lessons in Living," which taught her to do something about her attitude towards life. Day by day she made little gains, and today she has been advanced in her position because she has learned the secret of how to control those things in her which were negative and to develop those things which were positive. The general manager mentioned this to me because he and his company were so grateful for the great change for the better that had taken place in one of their older employees.

Every man and every woman wants happiness. We all want to have a dollar or two to spare. We all want power of some kind in order to overcome past failures. Therefore, we must first of all put to work every talent we have, great or small, that they may grow day by day as we learn to put more faith in that power within us that guides us and inspires us with new ideas and new confidence in our innate abilities. This is the power of God working through us by way of the Master, Jesus, when through faith we have let go our sense of separation from Him.

Some time ago a woman was left a widow with two children to look after. She had no money that Christmas to buy gifts for her friends and relatives, so she prayed earnestly for it. She prayed believing she was now receiving. One night she had a dream. She saw a Christmas tree filled with envelopes on the branches. As she looked at the envelopes, she saw that on each one was written the name of a friend or a relative. The next day she sat down and wrote nice letters to them, letters of sympathy to sick relatives, words of courage to an uncle faced with difficulties. She wrote ten letters of blessing. All her life she had never believed she could write in this way, yet she did.

One of her friends said afterwards that she had got a wonderful message from her letter and it had brought peace of mind to her. The uncle wrote that his troubles had been solved through her advice. What came to her in return? The greatest blessing of happiness that she had ever known. From then on she started to write, and today is a well-known columnist on an American newspaper.

The minister of a church I went to some years ago felt a great need for funds in his church but the congregation lived in a very poor section of the city. One Sunday he got the idea that he would take up the collection at the beginning of the service and asked all who had received blessings from God recently to give well—to God. He was amazed at the amount of money that was given that day.

In the Jewish faith and the Buddhist religion people are taught that before any member of their religion ever asks for a blessing of any kind from God, he must first of all sacrifice some material benefit for God.

Many people come to see me from day to day privately, asking for advice, for help, but many of them never remember to give anything to God for the benefits they are coming to receive. The world is filled with people who want something for nothing, who never realize that one of the basic laws of life is that we must give before we can get.

The Master said that he that findeth his life shall lose it, but he that loseth his life for His sake shall find it. What does this mean? Simply that he who gives his life in the service of his fellowman shall find it in so doing and shall reap abundant living.

Have you ever realized that what you keep to yourself you lose, and what you give away is yours forever?

During my life I have met many married couples who had made up their minds to keep up their business careers and refused to have a family. I have seen many of these couples grow rich, but almost invariably there was a reckoning, when one or the other, sometimes both of them, would come down with a very serious sickness requiring months of hospitalization. Where did their money go then? What they decided to keep for themselves they had lost.

During our earthly life God has to work through men and women, and He cannot be shut out. He must be expressed some way or other every day of our lives. All of us must come to the realization that we are inseparable from God.

What must we do to win that victory over defeat which is the goal of all humanity? What must we do first of all to gain spiritual supremacy? We must give and give freely of whatever we have in talents, or service, or money.

The farmer in the spring casts the seed into the ground. Then he covers it up with the earth and awaits the harvest. He waits in perfect faith believing that the law will work for him once more; although he has nothing to show you, he knows that it is on its way. And so, in the fertile soil of your mind, this law is just as dependable. Sow your good deeds, then cover them up and in due season your own will come back to you. This is how you lay up treasures in Heaven and they never fail to wing their way to you in time of need.

Have you recently told a story about someone which was not quite true or which was mean or unkind? Then look out, for this same law will bring back to you after its own kind; you will reap sorrow, sickness and trouble. When you do something to help someone else, then that something brings you closer to God, for in this way you allow yourself to be a channel or an outlet for God, and automatically you will reap what you have sown.

I met a young lady who had suffered from many sleepless nights and had no peace of mind. Eventually she developed a nervous breakdown. Years before it appeared, she had deliberately lied to her employer and now she was reaching middle age and was many years older than she had reported to her company. At this stage she felt she was about to be found out. When she spoke to me about it, I said, "Go to your manager direct and confess it. Tell him why you did it and what you have suffered."

She did this, and gained peace of mind and with it freedom from all her nervous trouble. Her manager very kindly and generously forgave her. She had been mentally picturing for months being discharged from her job and being unable to find another one

Many people think it is quite the right thing from time to time to get away with little lies, but every lie you tell means that later on in some way it will come back to you to cause you embarrassment or dismay.

Make a change in your pattern of thinking today. Take God as an active partner into your business, into your life. You need finances for that business. Say to Him, "Father, thank you for bringing to me what I need for my business." Then try to see how you can give better service to your customers, to your friends and relatives. Try to see how much more you can give financially to charitable organizations or to your church. You are rich according to your own kind of thinking.

Many business men have told me how grateful they were for the lessons they had learned from my lectures and literature. They had discovered for the first time the law of giving and, when they applied it, they reaped abundance.

We often read in books about the unpardonable sin. I have never had a reasonable interpretation given to me of this statement, but I personally think that if there is an unpardonable sin it is the damming up of God's powers within us by refusing to believe that His power is available to us every moment of our lives.

When you constantly suffer from sickness, you are lacking in faith. When you are surrounded with debts, those debts have come to you by your own wrong thinking, by your lack of understanding, and you are reaping exactly what you have sown; in other words, you have shut God out of your life in one way or another.

At a lecture recently a lady was present who had decided, on leaving, that she would place fifty cents in the love offering box. However, the lecture appealed to her so much she felt that she could not give that amount. She had to sacrifice, so she put a dollar bill in the box which was more than she thought she could afford.

She had a friend who had been trying to find a job, and the next morning an idea came to her at breakfast. She went into her room and prayed about it and acted upon the idea and succeeded in getting the person who needed it an excellent position. This was no coincidence. The sacrifice she made at that lecture opened the way for abundance to her fellowman, and in turn it has brought a more abundant life to this person.

She did not say in her mind, "If I give that dollar to God I want so and so for it." She did not say, "If I can get a position for so and so, I will make a sacrifice." No one can bribe God, at any time, but if you only knew this wonderful law of giving you would certainly operate it successfully every day because in so doing you open the door to divine love wherever you are, whoever you may be. This is God's way of doing things.

Why not start praying as you read this book if you are in trouble or in sorrow or in sickness. Don't expect an angel to suddenly appear to you in person, but know and believe with all your heart that God works through ordinary folk like you and me, and that it is through ordinary people that good will come to you.

Have you ever thought of the fact that God is willing to wipe out from your consciousness and your life all the things that have been wrong up to date? That you can come to a conviction right now that God's wealth, God's health and God's success are all yours for the taking? "I am come that they might have life, and that they might have it more abundantly."

The law of cause and effect simply means that whatever we think or do in life will come back to us in due course, returned with interest exactly in kind. We must invariably reap whatever we sow.

There Is No Death ⤳

"They shall hunger no more, neither thirst
any more . . . and God shall wipe away all
tears from their eyes."—*Revelations 7:16-17.*

THE Bible tells us that in our afterlife the beauties of that
world to which we go will be far greater than anything we
have ever seen before.

We have no conception whatsoever of the magnitude or
the greatness of the beauty that we shall see after we have
crossed the valley of the shadow. Every tear will be wiped
away from our eyes; no fears, no anxiety, no debts, no worries
of any sort at all shall beset us.

Something beautiful seems to come to people when they
come to the end of the road. I have seen the happy light in
the eyes of those who were passing on, leaving behind the
physical body.

As I sat at the bedside of my father who had been uncon-
scious for days, he suddenly looked up and recognized me and
the other members of the family. Then he read the text on
the wall beside him and he said, "I certainly do know that my

Redeemer liveth." He told us that all around his bed were his mother and father, his brothers and sisters who had gone on before and his face lit up with a holy light as he talked to them and he talked to us. Then suddenly he was gone.

Was this imagination? Certainly not! For a few moments he had hovered on the edge of that new life seeing the physical as well as the spiritual. This I have seen on many occasions. It is part of the goodness of God that after a lifetime of tribulation we can take up, if we wish, the joy of living with God forever and forever.

Are you certain of that joy in an afterlife? Could you write a letter to God today and say, ". . . faithfully yours." Will God say to you when your number is up, "faithful servant," or do you care?

The Bible teaches us that life on earth is but preparatory to that life of permanent happiness in Heaven to which all souls can go when the period of training is over. Whether you have been born to poverty or wealth, whether you have lived in the top ranks of society or the ranks of the poor, makes no difference whatsoever. But all of us go to that new life with one possession, our character.

The size of the house you live in, the money you have tried to accumulate, or the fortune you have made are all left behind because these things have no value when you come to the end of the road. You came into this world with nothing, and you leave it with nothing except your character and the lessons you have learned in life.

What handicaps have you overcome? What sins have you fought and won a victory over? Is this world a better place because you have lived in it? Is anyone happier because of your goodness to them? What have you done for Jesus Christ? All these things help to build your character and develop your soul. This is the purpose of your life on earth.

What is this separation called death? It is not death at all; there is no death. It is the gateway to eternal living, when we all get the rewards we have won through our faith, through our religion, through our belief in God, and Christ, His Son.

In the New Testament we read that Jesus said to one, "She is not dead but sleepeth." To another, "Lazarus sleepeth, but I go that I may awake him out of sleep." So Jesus looked upon death as really sleeping, for He taught us very definitely that the body is but the temporary home for the soul and that this thing called death is but graduation to another and far happier life.

Is this happy land to which we go located in some distant planet? Oh, dear, no! That life is right here and now around you every day that you live. It is simply a transference from a physical to a spiritual plane, each completely interwoven with the other. There never has been a beginning for God, and there will never be an ending. The continuity of your life is not interrupted by your death because there is no death to the soul who has found Christ.

The statement is made in the Bible that the soul that sinneth shall die. This means that if we die deliberately in sin, then we shall never see God. Could you dare take a chance of dying like this? Can you risk an eternity away from love, away from God, just because you preferred the thrills of your emotions, the material pleasures that the world provides, of money, of pride, and sins of all kinds. No one can take such a chance as that.

[155]

Yet you, and you alone, can say whether or not your soul shall see the beauties of Heaven . . . and God.

I have seen many people obsessed with a terrific fear of dying; and yet when they came to that final day they found it just a peaceful passing along the road. They got a glimpse of that brightness, a glimpse of their loved ones waiting for them to come over. Rest assured that there is someone there to meet you when you leave this plane.

When you came into this world the loving devoted hands of your mother were waiting to receive you; so, when you leave this world, loving hands, angelic beings, will be waiting to welcome you into that beautiful land where sorrow is no more.

We are apt to shed tears and to mourn about our loved ones, but as Christians with a real undaunted faith in Jesus Christ, we should never shed those tears, for that shows a lack of faith, and by holding fears for our loved ones we hold them back from progressing along the heavenly road.

If you are doing this at the present time, then release your loved ones and let them go. If your son should win a scholarship to a university and take his four years there free of cost to you, how happy you would be. Then look upon death as a scholarship into the highest school of all. So why should we fret and cry about it, why worry about it, why fear it?

Do not fear the coming of this crisis into your life; it is never a dark lonesome road to travel; it is filled with light and joy and happiness, and God wipes all tears from your eyes over there. The Chinese people wear white at their funerals to show their joy at the release of their relatives from a world of trials and sorrows. We should do the same thing for we know that our loved ones have won their great reward. If you have tried to live with Jesus Christ, then you too will win your reward, the greatest that can ever come into your life.

Through the whole of my life I have had many psychic experiences which have afforded me the opportunity to look into that other world beyond the veil. In my religious work, these experiences have grown from month to month, and during healing services I have seen many glorious sights. My psychic researches have taken away from me all fear of death because I know there is no death. It is a gateway to life everlasting.

A clergyman told me this story. While he was visiting a dying member of his flock, the man's dog scratched at the room door to be allowed to enter. The sick man said, "I am like my dog. He does not know what is in this room, for he has never been in it, but he knows I am here and that is good enough for him. He wants to come in. Just so, I do not know what is in the many mansions of Heaven, but I know Jesus Christ is there. That is enough for me; I ask no more of Heaven."

Many of the subjects I have given in my Bible class have been dictated to me by my loved ones long since passed on. This does not mean for one moment that I wish to be labeled as a spiritualist. In my psychic work I have seen the great danger of people who constantly try to look beyond the veil. We must remember that while we are surrounded by powers of good, we are also surrounded by thoughts of evil, and I know from experience that many a medium, in giving the answer to a problem, is simply tuning in on the subconscious mind of the individual. The message does not come from the spirit world.

It is not our purpose to deliberately spend our lives peeping into that other land, for when God wants us to see with our spiritual eyes, He will open those eyes and give us the lesson He wants us to learn.

In all my lessons I have taught that evil can never win a permanent victory over us. The much feared religion of communism may conquer the whole world, but it is basically evil and therefore will be overcome finally, and only good will prevail. The next few years may be very difficult ones for this world. But evil will be finally destroyed and false conceptions of its power along with it.

"I am the resurrection and the life. He that believeth in me . . . shall never die," said the Master. This teaches you that there is no death, for, when your soul awakes in that other world, you will have a more glorious body than you have ever owned. You will go to that plane of thought which you have prepared for yourself, and the more you learn God's laws, the more you progress.

Jesus said, "In my Father's house are many mansions," and I am sure He did not mean houses. He meant many planes of thought; and according to the way we have lived, so we will find ourselves. In that future life you will have a full memory of your past life. The character you have developed here will go with you, and the moment you arrive at that other shore, you will have angels to guide you and teach you how to get a greater consciousness of God. You will grow spiritually over there just as you did here.

The Holy Communion service of our church was developed through the centuries, a passing on of the teaching of Jesus when He gave this fellowship as a symbol on the night before He died. We are taught by that service that we join in a spiritual fellowship with God and all our loved ones who have gone before. I have found that this teaching gives the greatest confidence to those who are willing to accept it, for they can have that fellowship every hour of the day. They can actively associate with others who are living vital lives.

I do not think for one moment that God allows those who have preceded us to just look upon the sicknesses and sorrows which we have to undergo in this world, but I earnestly believe that at certain times in our lives, when good can be accomplished, they are allowed to intervene in human affairs.

The physical body is used as an instrument of the soul just as a fountain pen is used as an instrument by the mind. If you lose your pen you don't cry about it, you find another pen or pencil to write with. The loss of a pen does not silence you forever on what you wanted to write. As you go through life, no one sees your real person, they just see your physical body. As I preach in the pulpit you cannot see me, you only see the house I am occupying, you cannot see my sins, my virtues, my hopes. Yet what am I but the sum total of the component parts of my soul, which is indestructible and eternal?

I do not believe in the materialistic hell painted by the church of long ago. It is not a place of fire and brimstone, filled with little devils and their pitchforks. It is the place of complete separation from good, from God. Can you imagine a worse punishment, when you think of what you might have been, than the pangs of eternal remorse? This is far worse than material fire which, of course, could never harm you in a permanent way, because your spirit cannot burn.

The paradise to which we go at death is a place of rest and growth. Our loved ones in this realm are sent to help us along the path we now must travel, and their instructors are angelic beings. What are angels but thoughts, messengers of God?

The Bible teaches us that judgment comes to all of us after death, but none of us need fear that judgment if we have done our best, if we have tried to live with Christ, overcoming those things which are wrong in our lives. God will not condemn us to an eternity of hell for some misdeeds we had performed in our former life.

I was called to the bedside of a lady who was dying, and she had a great fear of death. Her family did not want to tell her there was no hope, but she had sensed it already; so I showed her the beauties of a Christian life, and she prayed very earnestly with me at her bedside. Immediately she lost her fear of death, and something seemed to tell me to pray fervently then for her recovery. So we prayed believing we were now receiving, and she made a most amazing recovery from the edge of the grave.

Today she is living a happy, healthful life. A better Christian I have never met, and she is now ready whenever the call comes to her. The end of the road does not mean termination to her, for she knows that divine beings are waiting on that other side to receive her.

What about you? Can you face God if He calls you home this very moment? If not, then it is time for you to think what you might have done in your life and what you still can do for God. Learn how to make your faith a realistic one. Make your religion live with you every hour of every day by putting God first in your life and make up your mind to live with Christ. If you do, you will gain an overcoming of everything, including death.

You will thirst no more and God will wipe all tears from your eyes, forever and forever.

There can't be death where God is, and God is everywhere!

What God Means to Me ⌒

AS A CHILD I had a very great fear of God. To me, He was a vengeful sort of person, always trying to catch me doing some wrong thing and then trying to punish me for so doing. I well remember the second commandment and what it meant to me, "For I the Lord thy God am a jealous God, visiting the iniquity of the fathers upon the children unto the third and fourth generation of them that hate me."

How terrifying was the Victorian picture of a sadistic God, and how wonderfully different is the picture of God given to us by Jesus Christ: a loving, merciful, devoted Father always willing to forgive His wayward children.

Throughout my life as an Episcopalian, I have certainly believed in the Christian aspect of God. I always realized my sinful ways, but I did not realize that His power was my power to use, that Christ lived within me, until after many years of illness, and then having but less than a year to live,

I discovered the God within, which has brought me many years of complete freedom from illness and has indeed given me life more abundantly.

Although, according to the teachings of my church, I had given myself to God at my confirmation, I really did not know Him in a true sense, nor did I have any idea that the healing power of Christ was now available to me. I believed that God forgave my sins—oh, yes; but I did not think He forgave and released me from sickness as well, if I would only believe. Many a time I prayed for healing, if it were His will, and when that healing did not come, then I accepted this, believing it was God's will for me to suffer sickness.

The reading of a book called *In Tune with the Infinite* brought me to a new conception of this Divine Being. This new idea I adopted and practiced daily, yes, hourly. Soon after this new life had begun, I came to a very real conversion at the radio in my study, after hearing an evangelist speak the word that was certainly meant for me that eventful day. On my knees I gave myself to God, thanking Him for my conversion and giving Him in all sincerity my heart and my devotion. Practicing my new-found faith hour by hour, daily overcoming temptations and fears, I found that my healing from many years of sinus, hay fever and stomach ulcer troubles had come. I found the Kingdom of Heaven within me and, oh, how my ideas of God changed.

Years of careful study and hourly prayer put me in constant touch with the Infinite, and daily demonstrations of my beliefs came to me. I gained the answer to my prayers and my viewpoint in life was completely changed. I learned and proved that Jesus Christ came to bring us a life more abundant. That i must live from day to day, resting in the consciousness of God's presence within me at all times. I went to the communion table of my church now with a new conviction, a new reality. I discovered it was a powerhouse for me, and I believed that in taking that sacrament I was indeed receiving strength and power to conquer all ills.

The more I studied the spiritual meaning of the New Testament, the more I got out of my faith. Then I came to a belief that God was the one creative power in the whole universe, at all times available to me for good. My Bible said that God was spirit and that they who worship Him must worship Him in spirit and in truth.

God to me is all life, all power, all love. You cannot see spirit, you cannot see love, you cannot see wisdom, yet these are all manifested in this Being, our loving Heavenly Father, called God. Wherever there is life, there also is God. They are inseparable. Every human being is the highest manifestation of divine creation, divine energy. Therefore is it any wonder that God, as told in Genesis, gave man dominion over all other things upon the earth?

Once I realized this, I suddenly came to the conviction that I had dominion over all germs. How could a cold draft give me a cold? How could getting my feet wet produce cold germs in my system? I refused to let such things have dominion over me. I realized that all food was God's food, so how could any food of any kind give me indigestion or stomach ulcers? I learned, oh, how truly, after years of suffering, that stomach ulcers come not from what we eat but from what is eating us, which means our worries, anxieties and resentments. Once I gave these up and refused to hold them in my thoughts, then came healing of body and soul.

God is the name given to that unchangeable principle

which is the source of all life, of all existence. As God He is impersonal, but as we come to know Him day by day as expressed in each one of us, He really becomes personal to us, a very personal, very loving Heavenly Father; and every person of every color and creed becomes a child of God when he learns to live in Christ and according to His teachings. Then verily indeed we all become sons of God, and we seek more and more for the good that is in us and we find more and more the good, the Christ, that is in every person whom previously we have disliked and resented.

My new-found faith in such a loving God brought to me daily proofs that He is indeed the giver of all good things, that He and I are always connected, that praying in faith is just like tuning in on a gigantic radio, and through that radio I can draw upon this power within me for all the good I want or need.

For the past few years I have indeed been blessed with a constant stream of answered prayers; all of them givers of joy and happiness. The more my prayers were answered, the more I wanted to spread the glorious message of what I had found myself. No longer would I ask God to heal someone "if it were His will"; it is always God's will to heal. I prayed believing that I was now receiving. I had complete and absolute faith, and have been able to pass on this faith to thousands of persons who have found release from suffering through it.

God means to me today "perfect everything," and the more I devote of my life to Him and His work, the more He shows Himself to me in everything I may do. We read in scientific books that there are thousands of lost arts in the world, completely forgotten, but the greatest of all these is the art of living as shown us by the Master. Yes, we recite creeds, we attend churches; but we have lost in the Christian church of today the art of living with Jesus Christ. Many of us found Jesus, yes, years ago, but oh, how easily have we lost Him in this maze of materialistic existence. Mary found Him in the temple where she had lost Him, and so, too, must we seek Him where we have lost Him, within our own consciousness, within our own selves!

Day by day I see the lives of men and women recreated by this Christ within. Each day I live I wonder at the goodness of the God I have come to love so much, when I see how easily and surely He forgives sinful living when the heart is opened to Him. This in itself is a miracle, indeed.

A man I heard of recently was in bed with a creeping paralysis for nine years, had lost the use of his legs and feet and toes, and had only partial use of his hands. I talked to him over a phone by his bedside. He did not know God at all; his life had been filled with making money. I taught him how to pray, believing, and we remembered him daily for the next week. When I went to see him the following week, he had the use of his hands, and his legs from the knees down. He came to Christ that day. That is what God means to me— Christ the forgiver, Christ the healer, God, all divine love.

A woman steeped in a lifetime of sinful living, and now at the point of suicide, came to see me asking for help. She had to be taught how real and how good this God I worshiped is. She asked forgiveness for her past life, she came to Christ, and was not only instantly released from her past evil life, but was cured of all her pain and ills. She is now rehabilitated, has an excellent job, and is steadily growing in grace with her new-found Christ within. This is what God means to me.

The art of living with Christ can be yours today if you are willing to pay the real price for it, taking up your cross, following in His footsteps, looking upon life as He looks upon it, and then reaping the reward of your Christian living with life more abundant.

For ages religion has been looked upon as a science rather than an art. We have taught it in precepts, in dogmas and in creeds; not in realities, not in absolute faith. Since the second century man has, through the church, formed varying dogmas, differing from century to century; hating, detesting those who differed, those who refused to accept them. In the Middle Ages the church devised devilish means of tortures to force its ideas upon those who refused to accept them. This was done in the name of a God of Love! Let us all try to find this Christ within so that we may all worship Him in spirit and in truth and that He may so fill our hearts that we all worship together in spite of our so-called differences.

The Kingdom of Heaven which I have found is the kingdom of human relationships, based on Jesus' teachings of two commandments whereby we put God first in our lives and our fellowman before ourselves. Believe in the power of the living Christ within you, let this sink deep into your mind and heart and soul, and you will also learn, as I have, what God can and will mean to you.

God has come to mean to me the source of all my supply, all my strength, all my happiness, all my needs, and my life itself. He has become my daily guide, my loving guard and pilot in everything that I do. I have come to love Jesus with an undying love, and with this increase of my faith has come the living in a spiritual world. My whole life then I devoted to the winning of souls for Jesus Christ. I am not merely interested in the healing of physical ills, but in bringing a new discovery of Christ to every man and woman I find who needs Him as I did. He lived and died for me; therefore I live for Him, and Him alone.

What does God mean to you, friend?

Healing by Faith ◠

W E ALL know only too well what the world owes to medical science and research, how doctors and nurses dedicate their lives to the healing of the sick. The cure of disease comes in many ways: by means of the doctor, the surgeon, medicines, good nursing, a change of climate But behind all these methods is this thing called faith.

Without the faith and will of the patient, medicines and doctors would be useless, for the factor which gives the victory lives within the patient, and this factor we must call faith. Within every man and every woman of every race and clime there is an instinctive "something," an instinct of the supernatural; this is what we call religion.

The stimulation of this instinct, often brought about by religious rituals and teachings, is no doubt responsible for many remarkable healings of so-called incurable illnesses.

Most physicians realize very well indeed what a decisive

part faith plays in the overcoming of sickness. This faith is activated from the mind, the intellect. If your heart and your head will share in a common real belief, the result is faith, and through faith all things are possible.

In the Christian Faith we have been taught but little about the power of thoughts, but it is absolute truth that the way we react to our thoughts and to our emotions affects every single cell and function of our bodies.

I have seen in my nutritional work how to produce certain diseases, called deficiency diseases, by taking from the diet of laboratory animals certain vitamins or minerals. I have also witnessed on many occasions what part fear, anger and nervous tension play in the health of such animals; but when we get a combination of such deficiencies together with these nervous tensions, the results in every case are death-dealing. We live in an age of processed foods, often completely lacking in the essential vitamins for our needs.

We live in an age of terrific tension, we rush about our daily work from morning to night, filled with fears, worries and anxieties. Is it any wonder therefore that in this present age we have so much physical and mental illness? These conditions are death-dealing to every one of us.

Every day in our individual lives we gain new experience, and it is in how we face these conditions, how we react to the events of each hour by thought and action, that we develop the patterns of our lives. If we live in the memories of yesterday, we are, so to speak, turned to salt; and if we live in fear and anticipation of a nebulous future, then, too, we shall be destroyed.

Have you ever realized that God placed a microbe in a drop of water and it lived and prospered in it? He gave an ant a little piece of ground and it lived victoriously. God gave the lion a forest and it became its king. But God gave man dominion over all things, and what has man done about it? He has the power of mind, the power of will and the gift of choice, yet man has closed his eyes to truth. Hence we have wars, famines, hatreds and diseases.

Year after year we read of the wonderful researches of medical science for the overcoming of many diseases, and the strenuous developments of surgical science. But, to me, the greatest of all healings are those of the Master, Jesus, when He said, "Go wash in the pool of Siloam," and sight was restored; "Go show yourselves to the priests," after the lepers were cleansed. All His life was a record of healings of incurable conditions.

These have by no means been impossible since His body was destroyed on Calvary and raised again. He lives, His Spirit is within you today, to heal and to give you the power to overcome all things. Every one of us resembles a Persian carpet, for each day we weave the carpet of our character by the thoughts we think and the things we do. You are where you are today by the experience of your past thinking and, as you believe, as you develop this thing called faith, you change the pattern of your living. You surrender to Christ the errors of the past, and His hands become your hands, His thoughts your thoughts, and you grow daily in the consciousness that Christ is now leading you into quiet waters.

Your body needs physical food every day it lives, but oh how much spiritual food your soul needs as you go about this problem of living. Only you, yourself, can develop these spiritual powers; only you can master the principles that operate these tremendous powers within you.

[171]

The whole of the universe is operated upon the laws which God has ordained. It is when we, through wrong thinking, through wrong living, attempt to break these laws, that we have to take the punishment that goes with an attempt to break any law. All sickness and unsuccessful living does not come from sin or error; we often have to suffer for the sins of others. Jesus never sinned, yet He suffered and died for the sins of the world.

Jesus never claimed to be different from other men. He said the things that He did we could do also. He told us that the Kingdom of Heaven was within us. The only thing that stops us from finding this kingdom is our lack of faith.

Jesus taught us that God was power, love, truth and life. Not just some of these essentials, but all power, all love, all truth and all life. He told us that the love of God was always at our command, and the way to gain that power was by simply believing, by having faith, by living according to the simple laws of God.

The woman who was healed, after years of incurable illness, by touching the hem of Jesus' garment, touched at that moment the principle of life itself. Touching wholeness brought her wholeness. This is available to every one of us today. We can and must come to Christ as she did, through the wrongs of our sins and errors. We, too, can touch Him and gain that healing for which we have so much real need.

God does not at any time withhold any good thing from us, His children. God is never vindictive. But the one who needs healing from hate and resentment, from a lack of belief in God, must first of all learn to love. To gain happiness, we must first of all give happiness to others.

The Bible says, "There is therefore now no condemnation to them which are in Christ," to those who live in conscious union with God, His spirit and His nature. I have never seen a miracle, yet I have seen thousands of wonderful, almost miraculous healings, from sin, error or sickness. Every single healing I have seen has been the logical, inevitable result of a cause set in motion when the patient came to Christ, when faith became the dominant factor in that person's life.

The punishments we get every day of our lives, the unhappinesses we gain, often the sicknesses we suffer, are the logical results of our acts and our thoughts of years before. When you learn to believe, when you learn to study spiritual principles, then you will see every day of your life things which you will deem miraculous.

"If thou canst believe, all things are possible to him that believeth."

A short time ago, with a clergyman, I visited the home of a man of sixty-three who was not expected to live more than another week. He had a serious heart ailment and was propped up in bed, finding it hard to get his breath. He had been a good Christian all his life, but he had given up hope. The doctor had told him the worst. I chatted with him for half an hour, then we prayed, thanking God for having begun his healing. He fell asleep and he slept for many hours. His healing had begun. The following afternoon he sat in front of his living room fire having tea, and the following Sunday was in church. The healing had been accomplished. His minister was shocked to see the rapid change. He had himself given up the man to death, for his prayers had not availed.

[173]

Why? He had prayed merely hoping, wishing; for he himself had never seen a healing by absolute faith.

Two parents came to me with a child of three, one day. The child had been injured at birth; the boy was dumb and could not use his legs at all. Otherwise he was perfect. I asked the parents if they held resentment towards the doctor whose instruments were supposed to have caused this. They said, "Yes." I then told them that God could not heal until they asked His forgiveness, and they were to see the doctor and ask his forgiveness also. This they promised to do. Then I prayed, thanking God for having begun the healing of the child. In ten days he had uttered several words, speaking well, and his legs came into use. Three months later I saw him running around and saying many, many words; he was healed. But God cannot heal if there is something in our lives blocking the power of faith.

This coming to Christ means that we must forget all our fears, all the wrong things we have held in our minds about life and about people. We need no university degrees to contact God, just simple faith and, if everyone could only realize how very simple it is to have faith, then they would never know fears again as long as they lived.

God's intelligence is available to your intelligence for use, for guidance and inspiration. He wants you to be a happy, successful, healthy person, and He is ever waiting for you to use His power through Jesus Christ. What is your relationship to God?

Is your religion merely a form, a series of rituals, a number of memorized prayers? Then that religion will never teach you absolute faith. You have but the shell, you have lost the kernel. It is the inside that counts, not the externals.

Jesus has told us that when we learn to be perfect in thought, word and deed, that if we really try day after day, then we will discover God. Every good thought you have, every good deed you do, every good secret desire of your heart is a whisper from God. Take time each hour of every day to contact God where you are, get an appointment with Him for one minute hourly, and day by day you will gain faith and conviction. Your thoughts, your whole personality, will change, for you will become, as Jesus, able to overcome all things in life.

Because God lives within you, then truth lives within you. His spirit is in you, His power is within you. Attend God every hour of your day, and the law of God will always work for you to bring you health, peace of mind and happiness.

You know you sometimes think yourself into unhappiness, into a depression. Do you know that you can also think yourself into gladness? It is by such thinking that you get well, that you prosper, that your prayers are always answered. Become the master of your own thinking. Stop thinking about how tough life is to you, stop thinking about the future and the past, think of God's riches and love, try to express such thoughts from day to day. You will become whatever you think.

You can have an Easter day every day of your life, you can be resurrected today from sickness, from sin and error, by lifting up your thoughts in absolute faith to God.

Some time ago a mother whom I knew came to tell me that she was to be turned out of her apartment and her goods sold to help pay eight hundred dollars in back rent. She had two sons, both of whom thought only of alcohol and wicked living. We prayed that God had now begun to heal her condi-

[175]

tion. I really believed that God would, of course, show us the way out. As she left my office a thought came to me to tell her to go and see the executor of her husband's will. I knew nothing of him or of the husband who had been dead for years. I have no idea how that thought came, except that it came from God. She went, and this man gave her, not loaned her, a check for one thousand dollars on condition that these sons no longer make their home with their mother.

Absolute faith took care of this deserving widow. God will take care of you and your troubles now in exactly the same manner.

The most wonderful thing to me in the Christian Faith is God's marvelous power for forgiveness. He is ever willing to forgive your past, no matter how vile it has been. If you want to gain happy, healthy living, start now to believe. Devote some time each day to God; read His textbook, the Bible; be regular in your church attendance; and leave all your fears and worries to Him, for He cares for you.

This is the only way to develop faith—faith that moves mountains of fears and troubles. God has never deserted you, but you have deserted God if you suffer in this world. The prodigal son returned home to find the most wonderful gifts he had ever received. The father had never deserted him at all, but he had separated himself from the father. So, friend, what about you? Are you not a prodigal son, too? Then take Jesus Christ at His word— Come to Him now, and He will give you rest. If you will only *let go and let God,* you can climb the steps to victorious living.